In *Killing Kryptonite*, John Bevere draws on his own struggles and dives into Scripture to write one of his most powerful books yet. With compassionate insight into our human weaknesses and personal temptations, John challenges us to draw closer to God and to be strengthened by His Spirit. Despite the discomfort of facing your faults, you will be encouraged, inspired, and elevated by this super book!

CHRIS HODGES

Senior Pastor, Church of the Highlands

Author of *Fresh Air* and *The Daniel Dilemma*

In *Killing Kryptonite*, John brilliantly combines love and truth as he takes us on a fascinating journey down a road rarely traveled. There is a way to discover the life that we all long for—but the answers may surprise you. Read this book today and find answers to questions you haven't been able to articulate.

MARK BATTERSON

New York Times best-selling author of *The Circle Maker*

Lead Pastor of National Community Church

John Bevere is a practical, relevant, modern-day prophet who shows us how to overcome sin by grace that empowers. In his new book, *Killing Kryptonite*, he reveals how we all have kryptonite in our lives that can only be overcome by the love of God. Thanks be to God for giving John this revelation!

ROBERT MORRIS

Founding Senior Pastor, Gateway Church, Dallas/Fort Worth, Texas

Best-selling author of *The Blessed Life, The God I Never Knew, Truly Free,* and *Frequency*

This message is an urgent plea for the body of Christ to refuse to settle for less than everything God has for them! I believe John's biblical insight and motive to help believers truly live for God will be life-changing for those who take it to heart.

JOYCE MEYER
Bible teacher and best-selling author

If you have ever felt like you aren't living the life you want—maybe it's because you're not. If you know there is something holding you back, you will love John Bevere's new book, *Killing Kryptonite*. John will help you get honest about anything you are putting ahead of God and His plan for your life. Grab this book, open your heart, and let God's Spirit kill whatever has been holding you back.

CRAIG GROESCHEL
Pastor of Life.Church
New York Times best-selling author

"Test yourselves to see if you are in the faith; examine yourselves!" (2 Cor. 13:5 NASB). My close friend John Bevere is wisely encouraging people to do this. Too often those who are a part of church life have substituted membership for the transformation that comes with a truly personal relationship with Christ. Nothing is a greater indication of a spiritual birth than recognizing that the Spirit of Jesus is in us, and we can't escape that reality or relationship.

JAMES ROBISON
Founder and President, LIFE Outreach International
Fort Worth, Texas

John is honestly one of my top three writers. If I were to hand my four children a stack of books to read, study, and live by, John's books would be at the top of that list. *Killing Kryptonite* is not *soft, watered down,* or *unclear!* I believe this book has the potential to change the course of the church in this day and age. It is one I would consider an anchor and a lifeline for this specific generation that is facing so much uncertainty. The way John brings clarity for what love and truth are is a lifesaver!

BRIAN JOHNSON

President of Bethel Music and Worship University (WorshipU)

Worship Pastor for Bethel Church

Killing Kryptonite exposes the enemy's greatest ploy to steal your strength and keep you from your destiny. In this book, John will challenge you to be aware of the enemy and equip you to fight back with the same Spirit that raised Jesus from the dead. You don't want to miss this one.

CHRISTINE CAINE

Founder, A21 and Propel Women

In *Killing Kryptonite,* John Bevere clearly demonstrates the strongholds that can prevent us from fulfilling our full potential in Christ. This book is powerful, direct, and will bring readers face to face with the kryptonite in their own lives.

JENTEZEN FRANKLIN

Senior Pastor, Free Chapel

New York Times best-selling author

John Bevere's *Killing Kryptonite* reveals areas that could be holding us back from living out God's calling for us. This book challenges and encourages us to experience God's divine nature and power in our lives.

ANDY DALTON

Quarterback of the Cincinnati Bengals, National Football League

John Bevere's revelations on biblical principles, teachings, and love for people have been building both the individual and the kingdom for decades.

His books reach the four corners of the earth, and his impact on lives is immeasurable. I am grateful for his friendship and ministry and his continued obedience to put pen to paper.

BRIAN HOUSTON
Founder and Global Senior Pastor, Hillsong Church

Convicting. Spirit-filled. Powerful. *Killing Kryptonite* shakes the slowly tightening stranglehold of familiar sin with a fervor stoked by grace and truth. I believe this book will help lead a generation where truth is relative and obedience is unheard of to delight in the God who settles for nothing less than our absolute best—freedom in and surrender to Him.

LOUIE GIGLIO
Pastor of Passion City Church, Founder of Passion Conferences
Author of *Goliath Must Fall*

As great as John Bevere's books have been, this one will catch many by surprise. It's not that he strays from his unique ability to address vital issues. It's quite the opposite. The grace upon his life to be profoundly relevant is refined even more in this writing. What will surprise many is how he uncovers something that's right under our noses, but goes completely unnoticed. To say this book is needed is a great understatement. *Killing Kryptonite* is essential reading for believers in this day and age.

BILL JOHNSON
Bethel Church, Redding, CA
Author of *God is Good*

KILLING
KRYPTONITE

KILLING KRYPTONITE

KRYPTONITE

**DESTROY WHAT
STEALS YOUR STRENGTH**

JOHN
BEVERE

BEST-SELLING AUTHOR OF
THE BAIT OF SATAN

KILLING KRYPTONITE
PUBLISHED BY MESSENGER INTERNATIONAL, INC.
PO Box 888
Palmer Lake, CO 80133
MessengerInternational.org

Printed in the United States of America.

ISBN 978-1-937558-11-6 (hardcover edition)
ISBN 978-1-937558-12-3 (electronic edition)
ISBN 978-1-937558-13-0 (international edition)
LCCN 2017908682

The following acronyms that appear in the text refer to these publications:
BDAG: Bauer, Walter, and Frederick W. Danker. A Greek-English lexicon of the New Testament and other early Christian literature. 3rd ed. Chicago, IL: Univ. of Chicago Press, 2000. Logos.

CHS: Lange, John Peter, D.D. Lange's Commentary on the Holy Scriptures. Charles Scribner's Sons; T&T Clark; Scribner, Armstrong & Co., 1867–1900. Logos.

CCE: Jamieson, Robert, A. R. Fausset, and David Brown. A commentary, critical and explanatory, on the whole Bible: with introduction to Old Testament literature, a pronouncing dictionary of Scripture proper names, tables of weights and measures, and an index to the entire Bible. Hartford, CT: S.S. Scranton Co., 1997. Logos.

CWSB: Zodhiates, Spiros, and Warren Baker, eds. Complete Word Study Bible (KJV). Chattanooga, TN: AMG, 2000. Logos.

WSNTDICT: Zodhiates, Spiros. The complete word study dictionary: New Testament. Chattanooga, TN: AMG Publishers, 1993. Logos.

WSOTDICT: Baker, Warren, and Eugene E. Carpenter. The complete word study dictionary: Old Testament. Chattanooga, TN: AMG Publishers, 2003. Logos.

LOUW-NIDA: Louw, Johannes P., and Eugene A. Nida. Greek-English lexicon of the New Testament, based on semantic domains. 2nd ed. Vol. 1. New York, NY: United Bible Societies, 1989. Logos.

Edited by Bruce Nygren, Addison Bevere, Nathanael White, Cory Emberson, and Victoria Newfield.
Cover design by Allan Nygren.

I dedicate this book to the team members
of Messenger International.

Together we've reached multiple millions with the gospel of Jesus
Christ by the grace of God. This couldn't be done
without your faith, talents, selfless giving, and hard work.
Lisa and I honor you, enjoy laboring with you, and look forward
to the Day when Jesus will eternally reward your faithful service.

What gives us hope and joy, and what will be
our proud reward and crown as we stand before our
Lord Jesus when He returns? It is you!
Yes, you are our pride and joy.
—1 THESSALONIANS 2:19–20

Thank you, Messenger Team 2017!

Abby Addison Alec Allan Andrew Arden Ashleigh Austin Bonnie
Casey Chris Daryl David Dina Edward Glen Heather Jessica L.
Jessica T. Joe Joel Justin C. Justin R. Kacee Katie Lauren Mary Matt
Rob Rosalee Sara Sasha Scott Tim E. Tim J. Travis Vanessa Vicky

CONTENTS

SECTION 4: ELIMINATING KRYPTONITE

ABOUT THIS BOOK

Killing Kryptonite may be read cover to cover just like any other book. I've also designed the chapters to be short, taking no more than ten to fifteen minutes to read. With each chapter, you will find a Take Action component that will help you apply that chapter's truths to your life. Please don't skip over these action steps—they are a vital part of this book's experience. For this reason, I recommend only reading one chapter each day. That way you can take the necessary action before moving to the next chapter.

In the back of this book, you'll also find discussion content for those of you who wish to use *Killing Kryptonite* in a group setting. I've also created an online course and physical study that parallel the content in this book. Both of these are great options if you'd like to go deeper into this subject. (There is more information on the course and study in the back of the book.)

If you're reading this book as part of the *Killing Kryptonite* study or course, I recommend that you watch or listen to each week's teaching and answer the discussion questions in the back of the book as a group. Then have each group member read the corresponding chapters before your next meeting.

Don't hesitate to reach out to me and my team at Messenger International if you have any questions.

Enjoy the journey!

John

INTRODUCTION

This may surprise you, but I've never wanted to stop writing a book so many times in my life, which I'll explain in a moment. But first, how does a book entitled *Killing Kryptonite* apply to followers of Christ? Allow me to give a quick explanation.

Most of us know the word "kryptonite" from the fictional story of Superman. What has practically become an American folktale was originally written by high school buddies Jerry Siegel and Joe Shuster and first published in a comic book in June 1938. The story line of a benevolent hero possessing superpowers was a perfect antidote in the time of Nazi tyranny. Superman's popularity grew exponentially and eventually was communicated not only in print, but also on radio and television and in blockbuster movies.

After a time, the stories grew a bit dull to audiences due to Superman's invulnerability. This motivated writers in the 1940s to introduce what was to become the famous substance called kryptonite—a compound from Superman's home planet that could neutralize his superhuman powers. Under the influence of kryptonite, Superman was no more powerful than a human being.

As Christians, there is a "kryptonite" that neutralizes our God-given power and character. What is it? How do we recognize it? How does it affect us individually and collectively? How does it hinder our effectiveness and our ability to reach the lost? What do we forfeit under its influence? Why is it so easily camouflaged? These are some of the questions addressed in this book.

This is the twentieth book I've written with the help and guidance of the Holy Spirit. As I mentioned, in the process of writing this one, I wanted to quit five or six times. One reason: It was bringing me face-to-face with issues I couldn't ignore in my own life. I had to ask myself, *Am I settling for living below what I'm created for? Are we, the collective church, truly experiencing God's presence and power to change our communities?* I actually woke up on a few occasions and uttered these words, "Father, I'm not sure I like this book. I want to quit writing it."

Each time I sensed a stern "No" from the Holy Spirit. Finally, on the last occurrence, He assured me this message will give vital insights to propel building healthy individuals, families, and churches globally. Its principles could change entire cities.

After this promise, I continued writing in faith. When I got to the final section of the book, the last seven chapters, the benefit came into clear view. Not only did I see the wisdom of this message, but I also saw the urgency. I now consider it to be one of the more important messages released under my name.

Now that I've mentioned the payoff at the end of the book, the temptation may be to immediately turn to the final section. Let me caution you—please don't. If you skip the first three sections, the impact of the fourth section will significantly diminish. This can be compared to walking into a movie during the final twenty minutes to view only the climactic scenes. The impact wouldn't be nearly as strong as if you had watched from the beginning. Those who watch from the beginning cry, shout, or celebrate. You, on the other hand, would wonder why the movie is even desirable.

This book comprises twenty-eight chapters in four sections containing seven chapters each. This is done intentionally to help readers who have busy lives. You can spend ten to fifteen minutes reading a chapter each day for four weeks. Or you can take a chapter a week for roughly a six-month read. Or you can read it however you normally read books. Our aim is to fit the message into whatever reading schedule is best for you.

Finally, this message needs to be viewed as a journey—one that gives protection from kryptonite and insights to influence your world. Before we begin, let's pray and ask the Holy Spirit to open our eyes to see the wisdom of heaven, which strengthens us to fulfill our destiny on earth.

Father, in Jesus's name, open my eyes, ears, and heart to see, hear, and perceive Your will for my life. Holy Spirit, teach me, deeply and profoundly, the ways of Jesus Christ as I read this message. I look to You as my Teacher. May You speak to me from every sentence of this book. And may my life be forever changed. Amen.

THE POWER OF ONE

SECTION 1

1

THE AVOIDED
QUESTION

A special note from the author:
Dear Reader, if you haven't done this already, I strongly recommend you
read the Introduction. It will help set up the message. Enjoy your journey!

Killing Kryptonite? Is this a book about Superman? No, but there are striking parallels between his story and our life of faith. Let's consider the similarities.

Superman isn't from this world; a child of God is not of this world.

He possesses supernatural powers that normal human beings don't possess; we are supernaturally empowered in ways those of this world are not.

He fights evil; we fight evil.

He protects and liberates those oppressed by villains; we guard the weak and set captives free.

He draws his strength from the sun; we draw our strength from the Son.

There's only one thing that can stop Superman: kryptonite—a fictional radioactive substance originally from his home planet. Likewise, there is a "kryptonite" that originated on our home planet that can neutralize a child of God. Oh yes, it didn't originate on earth but was formed where we come from. Kryptonite not only neutralized Superman's otherworldly abilities, but it also made him weaker than a mere human being. Our kryptonite does the same.

What is our kryptonite? Before uncovering its identity, I need to set up the story. Kryptonite's huge advantage over Superman is that it isn't easily recognizable, so he could come under its effects prior to identifying it. Even so, the believer's kryptonite is weakening both individuals and the body of Christ, and to many it is still not recognizable. The purpose of this book is to identify it, as well as uncover how to eliminate it and its effects on us as individuals and as a community. So let's begin with a question.

Greatest Desire

What is our greatest desire? I say "our" because if we're truthful, it's the same for each of us. Is it to be successful, to be the best in our field, to be popular, to be happily married, to enjoy great friendships, to be a part of a vibrant community, to enjoy good health, or to have enough resources to do anything we fancy?

Each of these is attractive and most are even necessary, but do they identify our greatest desire? Don't we know of people who have all of these things, yet still feel empty? Don't we hear stories of Hollywood actors, CEOs, professional athletes, government leaders, and others who've reached what society considers the pinnacle of success in life, and yet they still find themselves lacking something? In their emptiness, some turn to drugs, alcohol, exotic pursuits, or affairs. Still others turn to religion, new age spirituality, or occultism, hoping to fill the void that gnaws away at their insides.

If we're honest, deep inside we all know that there is more. The true satisfaction every man and woman longs for, whether they realize it or not, can only be found in an intimate relationship with our Creator. No matter what you think about God, He is your deepest yearning. The contentment and fulfillment all human beings seek can only be found in reuniting with our Creator.

The reality is that God has "planted eternity in the human heart" (Ecclesiastes 3:11). Unless deception has gotten the upper hand on us, we instinctively long in our hearts for the "King of eternity" (see 1 Timothy 1:17 AMPC). God's Word concerning every human being is:

> They know the truth about God because He has made it obvious
> to them. . . . Through everything God made, they can clearly
> see His invisible qualities—His eternal power and divine nature.
> (Romans 1:19–20)

God isn't unknown to any human being. If any man or woman is completely honest, they will admit that at one point in their life there was a deep longing to know God. All of us instinctively know that He's omniscient, omnipotent, and omnipresent.

All who have come into relationship with Him know His presence, power, splendor, and majesty are unfathomable and beyond comparison. He's so mighty that some of the most powerful beings in the universe, called seraphim, continually stand in awe in heaven and piercingly cry out to each other about His awesome greatness. These massive beings do this with such passion and strength that their voices shake the doorposts of an enormous arena in heaven that likely holds more than a billion beings.

God's wisdom, understanding, creativity, ingenuity, and knowledge are so vast they are unsearchable. For centuries, the smartest scientists have searched and studied the secrets of His creation and never fully comprehended its complexity and wonder.

No human being has yet to fathom or experience the fullness of His loving kindness, compassion, and tender mercies. There are no borders to His love.

After enjoying the privilege of relationship with Him for almost forty years, I just recently was completely overwhelmed again by the thought of our Creator rescuing us from the condemnation we brought upon ourselves. He gave us, mankind, all the authority to govern the earth, yet we gave it over to His archenemy, Satan, and his cohorts. God, knowing our treachery beforehand, both planned and was willing to pay the enormous price to pull us out of slavery and imprisonment. We condemned ourselves, but He gave Himself to free us. He did it without breaking His Word, which could only be done if He became a man.

Since God had given man the earth, He couldn't get it back as God—it would take the Son of man to reclaim it. This is the wisdom of Jesus being born of a virgin: He became one hundred percent man but since His Father was the Spirit of God, He was free from the enslaved nature humankind had fallen into. Jesus was God manifested in the flesh. He knew the horrendous suffering that would be involved in rescuing us, but He loved us so deeply and completely that He freely chose to pay the price for our freedom.

This entire book, and volumes more, could be written solely about His goodness, magnificent love, power, and majesty. But what motivates the writing of this book is another question.

The Avoided Question

Since we are the children of such an awesome God, simple logic would conclude we should experience an extraordinary life. It is not only sound logic, but Scripture also supports this reasoning. We are promised all of the following:

- His divine nature,
- unselfish character,
- unconditional love and forgiveness,
- joy and peace beyond description,

- supernatural power,
- well-being,
- vitality,
- health,
- safety and stability.

And this list is far from exhaustive—there's more. We are also promised:

- divine wisdom,
- knowledge,
- understanding,
- ingenuity,
- keen insight and creativity.

All of these are intended to produce fruitfulness and success in our endeavors. In short, we are promised the attributes found in heaven. Recall, Jesus emphatically declares that His kingdom is within us; therefore, His will should be done on earth as it is in heaven.

Yet these qualities don't seem to be manifesting on either a macro or individual level. If we are honest in our assessment, do we see a significant difference between the people of God and the people of the world? Do we followers of Jesus stand out? Do we shine as lights in the midst of a dark generation? Consider our divorce rate—is there a marked difference between the church and society? Do we suffer from envy, jealousy, gossip, strife, and divisions resulting in failed relationships? Do we see character, integrity, and morality that are dramatically different from the corruption of our nation? Is there a distinction between believers and unbelievers in our health and well-being? Do we have an abundance of resources? Are we able to meet the needs of others and proclaim His gospel to every person globally?

Does all of this sound too high and lofty? Consider that under the old covenant, there was a time when silver was as common as stone and was considered worthless because there was such a surplus (see 1 Kings 10:21, 27). On the contrary, now under the new covenant, I frequently encounter ministry leaders who struggle due to limited resources and pastors who desire to help their local communities but can't due to a lack of manpower, funds, and other resources. In both cases, is this "on earth as it is in heaven"?

Jesus promises that when we seek first His kingdom and His righteousness, everything we need will be given to us. Not once did a lack of resources keep Jesus from doing what He needed to do. Unfortunately, there have been extreme teachings in the church about wealth and prosperity. These unbalanced teachings have caused people to believe that abundance is a bad thing. But what are we to give if we have nothing?

When we let the pursuit of God's kingdom possess us, He entrusts us with the necessary possessions to advance His will on earth. God is not a bad leader—He doesn't ask His followers to do His will without giving them the necessary tools. And, even more important, God is a good Father. He wants to bless His children. But He doesn't want possessions to possess us. It's not money, but the "love of money" that is the root of all kinds of evil.

There was a time in ancient Israel when there was not one poor person in the entire nation. We read, "All of Judah and Israel lived in peace and safety. And from Dan in the north to Beersheba in the south, each family had its own home and garden" (1 Kings 4:25). Dan was the city furthest north in Israel and Beersheba was the city furthest south, so what this Scripture tells us is that in the entire nation, not one person had to be cared for—no individual or group needed government funding! What was going on that caused this type of abundance?

In fact, this was not an isolated occurrence. If we examine God's people in the Old Testament, there were many generations that flourished in an astonishing way—strong economically, socially, and militarily. They had an abundance of resources, food, and wealth. When they experienced military attacks, they weren't defeated, but on the contrary came out on top. Other nations marveled at the quality of life they enjoyed. And keep in mind that this was under the old covenant, which is inferior to the new covenant!

Jesus is the Mediator of a better covenant, which was established on better promises (see Hebrews 8:6). If we consider His life, we see government leaders, bureaucrats (tax collectors), noblemen, prostitutes, thieves, rich, poor—simply put, all types of people were drawn to Him. Jesus changed communities wherever He went. He never lacked what was necessary to meet any need. If any attacks came against His team, no permanent damage resulted, and often bad situations turned into amazing successes.

The members of the early church were referred to as, "These who have turned the world upside down" (Acts 17:6 NKJV). They too had no lack, for we read, "God's great blessing was upon them all. There were no needy people among them" (Acts 4:33–34). They were so unique that often they had to convince military officers or community leaders that they were not gods and should not be worshipped. Citizens of this world viewed them as the supermen and superwomen of their generation. They eliminated sickness and disease from those who suffered. They shone as bright lights in the midst of a dark generation.

Again, may I ask, do our lifestyles differ significantly from our society? Do our lives shine so brightly that we are viewed as distinguished people of God? Have we made excuses and altered our theology from what Scripture clearly teaches to explain why these promises were only meant for New Testament times and have since passed away? The New Testament writers give answers, but we avoid answering these difficult questions.

What if we really listened to what Scripture tells us?

I'm not pointing a finger here but only asking us to consider this question: Is this "Thy kingdom come, Thy will be done on earth as it is in heaven"? We cannot ignore Jesus's words, "'The kingdom of God is within you'" (Luke 17:21 NKJV). His kingdom is here, within the body of Christ.

Are we living in our generation as Jesus did in His? Aren't we instructed, "Those who say they live in God should live their lives as Jesus did" (1 John 2:6)?

Are we as effective as the early church was in reaching their world? Are we seeing entire regions hear the Word of God in just two years? (See Acts 19:10.) Remember, they didn't have the Internet, Facebook, other social media, television, or even radio. Yet every person—not just in a city or nation, but an entire region—heard the gospel.

Is this what we are experiencing? Let's be honest in our assessment.

We've avoided the elephant in the room by saying, "God doesn't move like this any longer." It's as if we've contoured the gospel to align with our condition. We seem to draw back from—at times even disdain—anything that promotes power, strength, success, abundance, fruitfulness, or health. We say such a message is extreme, unbalanced, and self-serving. In doing so, we actually protect ourselves from having to answer some hard questions and give ourselves an excuse for not impacting our world with the gospel.

So the question I pose about our ineffectiveness is one that many, if not all, of us ponder. But why aren't we asking it? Why aren't we seeking the answer? Could it be our hesitancy is because asking the question may uncover issues we aren't willing to deal with? But if we don't ask and act on the answers, we'll remain far below the level of life we're promised and called to.

After being in ministry now for more than thirty-five years and nearing the age of sixty, I'm ready and willing to address the question. In fact, I feel a divine urge to confront this issue. I believe if we honestly address this question from His Word, the fullness of life we've been called to will be unlocked.

If you, like me, would like answers, then let's go on this scriptural journey together. It won't be quick and it may sometimes be painful, similar to what occurs when a skilled surgeon performs a complex procedure.

The doctor cares for his patient and executes the necessary steps to save the patient's life.

The Holy Spirit cares more deeply for us than any surgeon, both on an individual and a corporate level. Keep this thought in mind during some of the more difficult chapters we encounter. The end result will be strength, health, life, love, and vitality. I believe the answers have the potential to change the course of our lives, communities, and this generation.

If you're with me, let's go!

TAKE ACTION

God warns us in James 1:22, "Do not merely listen to the Word, and so deceive yourselves. Do what it says" (NIV). This tells us that if we hear a word from God (from Scripture, the Holy Spirit, or someone giving sound teaching), but fail to act on it, we have actually deceived ourselves.

The proof that we believe something isn't when we agree with what someone teaches us, it's when we act on it. That's why these activations at the end of each chapter are so important. Each one is a helpful jumpstart for you to take immediate action that is focused on the truths revealed in the chapter you will have just read. The activations are brief and shouldn't take too long to complete.

If you take the time to do each one, you will get a lot more out of this book and experience much deeper transformation in your life.

III

Asking the avoided question can be like going to the dentist for a cavity filling, but we need to choose courage and face it in order to receive the long-term benefits.

How does your life stand out from the world? Would people say you live like Jesus? Don't shy away from this question; press into it. How would your life be different if you lived like Jesus? What habits would you break? How would it change the way you interact with the people who are regularly around you? What would be different about the way you live with your family?

Take time to write your thoughts to these questions. Use Scripture as your guide. This will give you a target to aim for. Once you have some answers written down, pray over them. Invite the Holy Spirit to highlight one thing from your answers that He is doing in your life right now. Ask Him to make that one thing come alive to you in a way that gives you power to change.

2

INTRODUCING KRYPTONITE

In our opening chapter, an *attempt* was made to discuss God's greatness. I use the word "attempt," because no matter how magnificent or elaborate the language we use, there is no coming close to depicting His grandeur. There is no one superior—no one even comes close in comparison. God has no rival or equal, and He will reign from eternity past to eternity future. He's awesome!

As His children, it makes perfect sense that our lives should reflect Him, and this is made clear in Scripture. God's Word declares, regarding His sons and daughters, "As He is, so are we in this world" (1 John 4:17 NKJV). John the apostle didn't say, "As He is, so we will be in the next life." No, John states that as He is, so are *we right now in this world*! That falls under the category of mind-blowing! Again we read,

> Because of His glory and excellence, He has given us great and precious promises. These are the promises that enable you to share *His divine nature*. (2 Peter 1:4)

Think of it. You and I have been given *His divine nature*. Not the nature of the most renowned human being on earth. No, rather, *God's* nature, and Peter ensures we don't misunderstand by adding the word "divine." The Greek word used here is *theios*, which is defined as "what is uniquely God's and proceeds from Him" (WSNTDICT). The word "nature" is the Greek word *phusis* and is defined as "to bring forth, essence, essential constitution and properties" (WSNTDICT). Put the two together and the meaning is, "These are the promises that enable you to share *what is uniquely God's essential constitution.*"

We truly are born of God!

It troubles me when ministers make a comment such as, "There is really no difference between a Christian and a sinner; Christians have just been forgiven." That's heresy and it does two horrible things: First, it demeans what God has done for us through Jesus and, second, it nullifies His promise, thereby keeping His people bound to this world's corruption that's created through fallen desires.

Even nature avoids such a heresy. Have you ever heard of a lion giving birth to a squirrel or a thoroughbred racehorse giving birth to an earthworm? We are born of God and are His offspring. We are told, "Beloved, *now* [not *later* when we arrive in heaven] we are children of God" (1 John 3:2 NKJV).

In light of being His beloved, we should manifest unselfish character, unconditional love, joy unspeakable, peace that passes understanding, supernatural power, well-being, vitality, creativity, divine wisdom, keen understanding, supreme knowledge, and perceptive insight—and this list is far from comprehensive! Scripture promises attributes such as these on many levels, so, again, my question is, "Why aren't we seeing this on either an individual or overall church level?"

Before I address this question and others that are similar, I want to prepare you for the process in this book. The next few chapters may seem negative and rough, but I promise that answers are coming and they are satisfying.

Consider this scenario: If a doctor properly diagnoses melanoma at

an early stage and gives the solution as a small outpatient surgical procedure, this development at first does seem negative. The patient may say to
himself, "What a downer. I have cancer! I don't want to hear about this or
go through the corrective measures to free myself from this disease. But
I'll do it to save my life." But consider the alternative: If the doctor ignores
the problem and merely coaches the patient to live a healthier lifestyle by
eating proper food, regular exercise, and having a positive, stress-free attitude, the melanoma will continue to grow until it eventually is inoperable
and causes death.

God loves us far too much not to diagnose what holds us back and
could even kill us. He knows what restrains us can't be coached away by a
more positive lifestyle. Rather, it has to be confronted and removed. He is
a Father deeply committed to our health and well-being.

So as you read the next chapters, keep in mind the diagnosis needs
to occur so the corrective procedure can be implemented. The ultimate
result will be the abundant reality painted in Scripture.

Addressing the Question

If His kingdom is within us, why isn't it being done on earth as it is in
heaven? Why were some Old Testament believers, who were part of an
"inferior" covenant, based on lesser promises, living in ways far above
what we witness today? Scripture repeatedly answers this question! One
of them is in Paul's letter to the Corinthians:

> That is why you should examine yourself before eating the bread
> and drinking the cup. For if you eat the bread or drink the cup
> without honoring the body of Christ, you are eating and drinking
> God's judgment upon yourself. *That is why many of you are weak
> and sick and some have even died.* But if we would examine our-
> selves, we would not be judged by God in this way. Yet when we are

judged by the Lord, we are being disciplined so that we will not be condemned along with the world. (1 Corinthians 11:28–32)

The irreverence of the Corinthians during the Lord's Supper is identified, but the resulting consequences aren't limited to just the specified actions, as many have presumed. In fact, the way they observed the Lord's Supper as a full-blown meal is quite different than our ceremonial approach in modern times. We'll see as our study progresses that the root issue, which brought the judgment, was their awareness of disobeying God, yet they did it anyway.

Three consequences are listed for their behavior—weakness, sickness, and physical death. The meaning of the latter two is clear, but what about the first? Some definitions of "weakness" are a lack of strength or robustness or being impotent and powerless. This word can refer to many different areas of life. Overall, it speaks to the powerlessness to be who we've been created to be.

Let's revert back to Superman. The substance that was dangerous only to him—it removed his strength and rendered him powerless—was kryptonite. Superman had abilities that were otherworldly. He was able to do supernatural feats and possessed paranormal knowledge, keen sensory awareness, extraordinary power, and unwavering character. However, if exposed to kryptonite, Superman became sick and weak—even weaker than the average human being. If exposed to it over a long period of time, he could even die.

In essence, the apostle Paul is identifying the church's kryptonite. It weakens us, keeping us from walking in the power of the divine nature.

King David admitted a time in which he didn't repent and confess his sin, lamenting, "My strength evaporated like water in the summer heat" (Psalm 32:4). *The Message* Bible paraphrase records his words as, "All the juices of my life dried up." Another verse reads, "Sin has drained my strength; I am wasting away from within" (Psalm 31:10).

James states it this way: "Sin, when it is full-grown, brings forth death.

Do not be deceived, my beloved brethren" (James 1:15–16 NKJV). James is clearly speaking to believers and warns us to not be tricked by sin's power. If sin is not dealt with, it can do to the believer what kryptonite could do to Superman, even to the point of death. Following suit, Paul, as a loving spiritual father, warns the Corinthian church—and us—of spiritual kryptonite's effects.

A Strong Word of Caution

The first thing to emphasize regarding these challenging verses should be a word of caution. Paul does not say, "This is *the* cause for any weakness, sickness, or premature death among you." In other words, he is not saying that all hardships, sicknesses, and deaths are attributed to sin. Often we believers battle difficult situations because we live in a fallen world and there are real natural and demonic forces to contend with.

For example, there was an incident when Jesus and the disciples came upon a man who had been born blind. The disciples asked, "Who sinned, this man or his parents, that he was born blind?" (John 9:2 NKJV). Their reasoning assumed that the only way this man could have gotten this bum deal was due to sin.

Jesus immediately responds, "It was not because of his sins or his parents' sins." Jesus rapidly and decisively cut off this incorrect and horrible mindset. All sickness, weakness, or premature death is not due to sin.

It is the same mentality that fueled Eliphaz, Bildad, and Zophar's criticism of Job. Their accusations pointed to the cause of Job's suffering being his sins (see Job 5:17; 8:4–6; 11:13–15; 22:1–11). Yet just before Job's troubles began, God boasted that he was "'the finest man in all the earth. He is blameless—a man of complete integrity'" (Job 1:8). Job's suffering had nothing to do with his sin or lack of integrity. God stayed silent for some time but eventually said to Eliphaz, "'I am angry with you and your two friends, for you have not spoken accurately about Me'" (Job 42:7). When

God is represented as disciplining or punishing someone for sin, when indeed He isn't, it is a serious accusation against His character.

Years ago when I was a young believer, in many church circles people were judged to have sinned if they were facing hardships. This mindset still exists among some people, but fortunately not on a wide-scale basis as it did before. Biblical teaching and great leadership have eliminated much of this error in the church. The manner in which some have been spoken to out of this mentality is extremely distasteful, condemning, and even hateful. Sadly, this teaching has even turned some people away from the faith.

On the flip side, we must also remember Jesus's words to the man who was healed of his thirty-eight-year infirmity, "'See, you have been made well. Sin no more, lest a worse thing come upon you'" (John 5:14 NKJV). There is no denying the fact that Jesus affirms that sin opens the door to consequences and hardship. Jesus loved this man enough to lay His life down for him. Out of His fervent love for him, Jesus offered this warning.

We lack true love when we avoid addressing issues like these. In our staying clear of any behavior that could be mistaken as mean, accusatory, or condemning, we often swing the pendulum to the other side by not saying anything at all. Yet we still have the condition Paul describes of many being powerless, sick, and dying before they should. Is this love? Is this truly caring?

We have answers for others, but we avoid expressing them because we don't want to be misunderstood. So let's be honest: Where is the focus of our love? Do we love the church as Jesus and Paul did in speaking the truth to them? Or are we focused on ourselves, our reputation, possibly losing our following, or being misunderstood?

My Journey

In my early years of ministry, I was consistently encouraging and over-the-top positive with everyone in my world. I avoided confrontation like the plague. I even lied at times to avoid it and instead would say something uplifting. It was said about John Bevere, "He is so kind—he is one of the most loving men in the entire church." These statements got back to me, and I reveled in them.

In prayer one day, God spoke to me: "People say that you are one of the most loving men in the church, don't they?"

I responded, "Yes, they do." I would have thought God was pleased, but the way the Holy Spirit asked this question carried the signal that it wasn't going that direction.

The next statement affirmed my concern. He said, "Son, you don't love the people in this church."

In shock, I retorted, "What? But I do and that's what the people are saying."

He then said, "Do you know why you only use positive, uplifting, and encouraging words when you speak?"

"Why?" I cautiously asked.

"Because you fear their rejection," He responded.

I was floored. I was undone, at a loss for words.

"If you really loved people," He continued, "you would tell them the truth, even if you know there is a good possibility they'll reject what you say and even reject you."

It was a life-defining moment. I immediately changed, but then I swung the pendulum to the other side. I now spoke truth but lacked tact and tenderness, because I still lacked the most important ingredient: *true love*. I was traveling and ministering in smaller churches and, sadly, beating up the sheep. In looking back, I feel sorry for the people I scolded with no encouragement, as well as their pastors who had to clean up my messes.

In 2001, I ministered at a large conference held in a massive church in Europe. A few months afterward, I heard from sources on three different continents that this church's pastor had told influential leaders that I was harsh and beat the sheep. He was right.

This devastating news drove me to my knees. I prayed—rather, I cried out—like never before that God would fill my heart with His love and compassion for His people. He did. I came to know and understand for the first time in my life what it meant to truly love the people I ministered to.

Not Some, but Many

Keep this in mind: Paul passionately loved the Corinthian church. Evidence of this is when he writes, "Why? Because I don't love you? God knows that I do" (2 Corinthians 11:11).

In another part of the same letter, he writes, "For out of much affliction and anguish of heart I wrote to you, with many tears, not that you should be grieved, but that you might know the love which I have so abundantly for you" (2 Corinthians 2:4 NKJV). This church misunderstood him. They viewed his corrections and warnings as signs of a lack of love, and surely this can be the case in a church or other setting. There are many who are as I was: stern, harsh, and dogmatic, and lacking genuine love, care, and compassion. They may be strong and make bold statements, but from the motive of wanting to be right. Many have been a victim of such an abuse of authority. However, this doesn't make all correction and warning similar. Paul's words at times were strong, corrective, and rebuking, but they all came out of a heart of passionate love.

Along the same lines, Paul later writes, "I will gladly spend myself and all I have for you, even though it seems that the more I love you, the less you love me" (2 Corinthians 12:15). His frustration is evident. His love and deep concern for their well-being is misunderstood, and he's now viewed as a harsh leader—one who wants to keep them under the rules, so to speak.

So please realize that Paul's words, though strong in telling these dear ones the cause of many being weak, struggling with health problems, and dying prematurely, are out of his fervent love for them.

It would have been much easier to swallow if he had said "some," but he specifically says "many." How can we avoid facing the truth he's communicating? If it applied to them, does it apply to us? Would God put this in the Scripture if it were an isolated incident? Shouldn't it apply to us today? The answer is undoubtedly "yes."

One final point: Paul is not just addressing the act of communion in a church setting. There is so much more to what is being said, and many of us—myself included for years—have missed the overall message. We'll dive further into the meaning of his words in the next chapter.

TAKE ACTION

Go back and reread the beginning of the chapter to remind yourself of what's possible. Remember, you are called by this declaration, "As He is, so are we in this world" (1 John 4:17 NKJV). You are called by God to live as Jesus in your life right now, not someday in the next life.

How does that reframe the way you think about your daily life? Perhaps you wouldn't have thought of yourself as weak before understanding your potential in Christ, but now that you do, would you consider yourself weak or strong? If weak, you've assessed wisely. For God says that His power works best in our weakness (see 2 Corinthians 12:9).

God will only turn our weaknesses into strength when we humble ourselves before Him (see 1 Peter 5:5). Ask God to speak to you about any reasons for weakness in your life. Write them down and then ask Him for the keys to freedom from each one. Take time to write down God's prescription for turning each weakness into strength.

3

ONE

Let's revisit the apostle Paul's words to the church he loves:

> That is why you should examine yourself before eating the bread and drinking the cup. For if you eat the bread or drink the cup *without honoring the body of Christ*, you are eating and drinking God's judgment upon yourself. That is why many of you are weak and sick and some have even died. But if we would examine ourselves, we would not be judged by God in this way. (1 Corinthians 11:28–31)

In this chapter we'll focus on Paul's words, "without honoring the body of Christ." There are two things of immediate interest that I want to point out: First, he's not speaking to individuals, but rather to everyone in this church, which would be the community of believers in the city of Corinth.

In the past several decades, much emphasis has been placed on our personal relationship with Jesus Christ. Of course, this is a very important and real aspect of Christianity. However, what hasn't been stressed to the same degree is the corporate reality of being one body. Simply put, we are all one in Christ. It's important to keep both truths in view without neglecting one or the other.

Second, the NKJV translates Paul's words a little differently. It reads that the cause for many being weak, sick, and dying prematurely is due to "not discerning the Lord's body" (verse 29). Examining both versions helps bring a clearer picture to what's being communicated.

To gain insight, we have to turn back one chapter in 1 Corinthians where Paul discusses Israel's deliverance from Egypt and their time in the wilderness. In the midst of his discussion, he clarifies the purpose of bringing this story to their attention: "These things happened to them as examples for us. They were written down to *warn us* who live at the end of the age" (1 Corinthians 10:11). Paul is not merely giving a history lesson, but rather is issuing a present-day warning to protect us from certain judgment.

In discussing Israel's wilderness experience, the apostle opens up by illustrating their covenant relationship with God. He states that *all* were led by the Spirit of God (the cloud), *all* were delivered from Egypt (a type of the world), *all* were baptized (we were baptized into one body), *all* ate the same spiritual food, and *all* drank the same spiritual water (the Word of God)— the obvious emphasis is the word *all*. Then he summarizes by saying the rock that traveled with them was Christ. His point is clear: They were one body and they all belonged to one covenant-keeping God. This certainly correlates to who we are as the body of Christ.

Paul then makes the heartbreaking statement, "God was not pleased with most of them, and their bodies were scattered in the wilderness" (10:5). God loves us deeply, more deeply than can be comprehended. The truth is we can never do anything to cause Him to love us any more or any less. With this being said, however, it is important to point out that we are in charge of how *pleased* He is with us. This is why Paul states in another Scripture verse that "our goal is to please Him" (2 Corinthians 5:9). This should be a supreme goal for you and me and every believer.

Why did these Old Testament people die outside of the promises God made to them? Paul reports five sins that were the cause of their downfall: coveting (intently desiring something not of God or outside His provision), worshiping idols, sexual immorality, testing God, and complaining. A few verses later, Paul writes:

> You are reasonable people. Decide for yourselves if what I am saying is true. When we bless the cup at the Lord's Table, aren't we sharing in the blood of Christ? And when we break the bread, aren't we sharing in the body of Christ? And *though we are many*, we all eat from one loaf of bread, showing that *we are one body*. Think about the people of Israel. Weren't they *united* by eating the sacrifices at the altar? (1 Corinthians 10:15–18)

So here Paul again discusses communion or the Lord's Supper and gives us the bigger picture of the specific problem he mentions in chapter 11 of 1 Corinthians: *not discerning the Lord's body*. He acknowledges that we are *many*—many different individuals and we each have a personal relationship with God through Jesus Christ. However, on another level, in God's eyes we are *one*. This is the focal point of what Paul's saying. We are *one body* of Christ; we are *united* as Israel was.

So now we need to ask, "Was the judgment of being weak, sick, and dying prematurely assigned to each individual who was sinning, or was the body of Christ in Corinth as a whole suffering these consequences due to the behavior of some of its members?" Don't get me wrong—and I want to strongly emphasize this point: There are personal consequences for known practiced sin, but here we need to stay focused on the truth he's revealing. He is addressing the believers as a body, as a church, as one united people.

In this case, it's the body of Christ in the city of Corinth.

One Man's Act of Covetousness

Let's return to the Israelites who are examples to us. However, let's advance one generation to the one led by Joshua. This body of believers boldly crossed the Jordan River and marched into their promised land. Their first assignment was to destroy the enormous city of Jericho. No doubt a daunting task, but God would certainly once again show His mighty strength. There were specific instructions God gave to Joshua, one of them being,

> "Jericho and everything in it must be completely destroyed as an
> offering to the Lord. . . . Do not take any of the things set apart
> for destruction . . . . Everything made from silver, gold, bronze, or
> iron is sacred to the Lord and must be brought into His treasury."
> (Joshua 6:17–19)

All the spoils from Jericho were to be dedicated to the Lord's treasury. It was solely His, and none was for individual gain.

The attack came and the Israelites were invincible. They completely annihilated everything in the city with their swords—men and women, both young and old, cattle, sheep, goats, and donkeys. Then they burned the city and everything in it, except the gold, silver, bronze, and iron that were kept for the Lord's treasury. Amazingly, not one Israelite was killed or wounded.

We must remember that this is one of the cities that the previous generation had spied out, with the intelligence report revealing to Moses, "The people living there are powerful, and their towns are large and fortified" (Numbers 13:28). Now it was that prior generation's grown children who attacked this fortified city, and they demolished it with no casualties. Israel was supernaturally empowered. However, we read:

> But *Israel* violated the instructions about the things set apart for
> the Lord. A man named Achan had stolen some of these dedicated
> things, so the Lord was very angry with the *Israelites*. (Joshua 7:1)

Notice the Scripture does not say, "But *a man named Achan* violated the instructions." No, it reads, "*Israel* violated the instructions"! And, interestingly, it also states, "the Lord was very angry with the *Israelites*." It doesn't say "the Lord was very angry with *Achan*." Israel was united as one, and when one member sinned by violating God's instructions in coveting, responsibility was ascribed to all of Israel.

The tragic consequence becomes evident shortly after. The next city targeted was Ai. It was much smaller, so the team leaders said, "'There's no need for all of us to go up there; it won't take more than two or three thousand men to attack Ai. Since there are so few of them, don't make all our people struggle to go up there.' So approximately 3,000 warriors were sent" (Joshua 7:3–4).

Approximately six hundred thousand warriors had been involved in the battle of Jericho. This shows how insignificant Ai was in comparison. However, we read:

> But they were soundly defeated. The men of Ai chased the Isra-
> elites from the town gate as far as the quarries, and they killed
> about thirty-six who were retreating down the slope. (Joshua
> 7:4–5)

Is this the same nation that had just destroyed, with no casualties, the more significant and powerful city of Jericho? Yet now the warriors are weak, retreating, and soundly defeated. They've been exposed to kryptonite.

Tragically, thirty-six are killed—whereas at Jericho they were not weak, none retreated, and no one was injured or killed!

Let's ponder this: Achan sinned, yet nothing happened to him or his family. On the other hand after the battle at Ai, seventy-two moms and dads had no son return from this battle, thirty-six wives had no husband return, and a slew of children had no dad come home. It was not due to what their son, husband, or father had done—they didn't sin. Rather, it was due to what another man of another family had done!

Israel was now paralyzed with fear. Joshua and all the leaders fell on their faces before God. Can you picture this? They are confused, baffled, and crying out, "Why did You bring us across the Jordan River if You are going to let the Amorites kill us?" (Joshua 7:7).

Hear God's response: "Get up! Why are you lying on your face like this? *Israel* has sinned and broken My covenant!" (Joshua 7:10–11).

God doesn't say, "There is a man who has sinned among you!" No, He again declares, "Israel has sinned!" No one knew Achan had sinned. No one was party to his covetousness. Yet as an entire body they suffered from spiritual kryptonite. Joshua finds out who it was and confronts Achan, who responds:

> "It is true! I have sinned against the LORD, the God of Israel.
> Among the plunder I saw a beautiful robe from Babylon, 200
> silver coins, and a bar of gold weighing more than a pound. I
> wanted them so much that I took them." (Joshua 7:20–21)

Joshua and the leaders dealt swiftly with Achan's offense and once they did, we read, "So the Lord was no longer angry" (Joshua 7:26).

An Example

This Old Testament incident illustrates Paul's message to the church in Corinth. He writes, "That is why many of you are weak and sick and some have even died." We will discover in the next chapter that the sin being committed by some was affecting the church overall, not merely the individuals involved in the offense.

Have you privately questioned why so many believers in our churches today are weak, suffering from persistent sicknesses and diseases? These dear ones can't seem to get healed of these ailments, and some are even dying prematurely. Why are there so many single moms in our fellowships on food stamps, struggling to make ends meet? Why are so many believers unemployed or living on shoestring budgets and dependent on the government?

The list of struggles that can't seem to be overcome due to our weakness is almost endless.

In the days of Solomon, there wasn't one person on welfare or unemployment. In the book of Acts, there was no lack and people were readily healed of ailments, diseases, and infirmities. Why aren't we seeing this today? Could it be the practiced sin of some is affecting the lives of many others? Could we be seeing what Israel experienced with Ai?

Again, it is important to stress that there are personal consequences for known practiced sin. Achan ultimately suffered judgment, but Israel as a whole also encountered spiritual kryptonite from his sin. It is my hope that as we continue this investigation, your awareness of being part of a body grows equally as strong as your individual relationship with Jesus, and that you realize your actions as one member can bring either blessings or consequences to other parts of the body.

Before closing, I want to again stress that when we deal with liberating truths often it can seem negative, and the thought of *why even bring this up?* can easily creep in. But, ultimately, when truth is revealed, it liberates and brings freedom where there were previously hindrances.

In Jesus's words, "'And you will know the truth, and the truth will set you free'" (John 8:32).

TAKE ACTION

Perhaps you have seen the movie *Gladiator* and remember hearing General Maximus shout, "Stay together! As one!" and you saw the victories that strategy brought. It's no secret that the most effective military strategy is divide and conquer.

Jesus knew this well and taught that a house divided against itself cannot stand (see Matthew 12:25). When the body of Christ is divided in its loyalties to Christ, it is weakened as a whole. This means that one of the greatest things you can do for the worldwide impact of the church is to live your own life wholly devoted to Jesus's cause. This means dedicating all your regular, everyday activities to God as worship to Him.

God wants your whole life, not just your Sunday mornings. If you are not living your entire life—work, family, hobbies, etc.—as worship to God, repent today. Ask Jesus to give you vision for what a lifestyle of worship looks like in your life. Write down what He shows or tells you and ask God's Spirit to fill you afresh as you dedicate yourself fully to Him.

4

CONTAGIOUS KRYPTONITE

The way God designed our bodies is a model for understanding our lives together as a church. (1 Corinthians 12:25 MSG)

Think about your body and how all parts are essentially connected, even if they're not in close proximity. Your little toe is connected to your nose, your liver is connected to your knees, your mouth is connected to your spinal cord, and the list continues. There is no part that can survive separate from the other parts. Otherwise, it wouldn't be a member of your body.

If one part hurts, don't all the members suffer with it? If someone comes down with the flu or a virus, the sickness eventually inhibits his or her entire body with a loss of appetite, declining strength, clouded thoughts, and aches and pains. On the other hand, if one part is honored, all the parts rejoice. If a person receives a back or scalp massage, the entire body feels the tension relief and pleasure. The whole body loves what's happening.

We as a church are one. Israel, who is our example, was one, and Achan's willful sin affected not just him but the entire community. Israel was invincible in fighting against Jericho but just a few days later, the same nation's army was weak, soundly defeated, retreated from its enemy, and experienced terrible casualties. Figuratively speaking, the nation came under the influence of spiritual kryptonite. Is this what the Corinthian church was experiencing? A closer examination yields the answer.

As briefly stated before, the Lord's Supper in the early church was quite different than in modern times. Theirs was a meal and ours is more of a ceremony. So in context, their specific behavior Paul addresses is different than anything we'd encounter today. However, the root of their conduct is what's important.

Their specific situation was that certain individuals in the Corinthian church were not waiting for the arrival of all the members. Those who arrived early were feasting and drinking, most likely on the best food and wine, while the others who arrived later were getting the scraps. Many Bible scholars and historians believe it was the poorer or lower class that was neglected. Now read Paul's words:

> For *some* of you hurry to eat your own meal without sharing with others. As a result, some go hungry while others get drunk . . . . For if you eat the bread or drink the cup without honoring the body of Christ, you are eating and drinking God's judgment upon yourself. That is why *many* of you are weak and sick and some have even died. (1 Corinthians 11:21, 29–30)

Look at the two words I've highlighted in the above Scripture, *some* and *many*. It's clear, Paul discusses the sin of *some* (verse 21), yet the resulting consequence are that *many* are weak, sick, and are dying prematurely (verse 30). It's no different than Achan's incident; several who were not intentionally disobeying divine instructions were experiencing the consequences of the judgment of one man's known disobedience.

The *Pillar New Testament Commentary* states:

It should not be assumed that the sick or dying were particularly guilty of the sin, but, like most plagues of divine judgment in the Old Testament, the plague could fall indiscriminately on the community as a whole.

A Similar Incident

Earlier in Paul's letter, he addresses yet a different type of sin that also was affecting the entire community. He starts by saying, "I can hardly believe the report about the sexual immorality going on among you" (1 Corinthians 5:1). The situation was a man, who professed to be a follower of Jesus Christ—a child of God, a brother in Christ, and a member of the body of Christ—was living in willful sexual sin.

Paul's correction was not directed only to the man committing the sin. The church community acknowledged him as a brother and member of the church, yet the leadership was not addressing his sin but looking the other way.

Why were they ignoring his behavior? Most likely they didn't want to offend him by confronting his sin. Perhaps he was an influential man, a community leader, a popular athlete, or a huge tither. Corinth was a large, influential city and a center for the arts. It's possible he was an admired actor in their version of Hollywood, or a popular musician who had hit the charts, or a vocalist who was a key part of their worship team. The text doesn't tell us but we can assume that if he left, it would hinder their progress.

There could have been other reasons. Maybe they thought that if he left, he wouldn't hear the Word of God any longer. They may have reasoned, "It's better that he's in our fellowship hearing the gospel than in the world not hearing." It's possible their overriding mission as a church was to get attendees back to the next service, and confronting him would thwart that goal. Another possibility could have been the reasoning, "He's a baby Christian; let's give him time." I'm sure they hoped he would eventually "get it" and walk away from his sin.

Paul adamantly tells the leadership of the Corinthian church that they should remove this man. Let me list his statements:

- You should remove this man from your fellowship.
  (1 Corinthians 5:2)
- You must throw this man out. (1 Corinthians 5:5)
- Get rid of the old "yeast" by removing this wicked person
  from among you. (1 Corinthians 5:7)
- "You must remove the evil person from among you."
  (1 Corinthians 5:13)

Paul lowers the boom four times in one small chapter! Think about it—in just thirteen verses the apostle commands this group four times to remove this man from the church, and at one point even bluntly states, "You must throw this man out." That's strong! Remember, Paul loves this church and he also loves this man.

You may question, "Really, he loves this man? No way!" But in fact, we know he loves this man, because nothing can be written in Scripture outside the motive of love. For God inspires all Scripture and God is love (see 2 Timothy 3:16 and 1 John 4:8).

Please remember, this is not just spoken to the leaders of Corinth, but the entire church. Paul consistently instructed for his letters to be read to all the churches. Why is Paul so adamant and blunt about this? The answer is found in this statement, "Don't you realize that this sin is like a little yeast that spreads through the whole batch of dough?" (1 Corinthians 5:6). Once again, we see the entire community would be affected, not just this individual man. Read what follows:

> Get rid of the old "yeast" by removing this wicked person from
> among you. Then you will be like a fresh batch of dough made
> without yeast, which is what you really are. Christ, our *Passover*

Lamb, has been sacrificed for us. So let us celebrate the festival, not with the old bread of wickedness and evil, but with the new bread of sincerity and truth. (1 Corinthians 5:7–8)

Paul is back to discussing the central theme of communion. Israel's feast of Passover revolved around a sacrificial lamb. Even so, Jesus is our spotless sacrificial Lamb. As the first Passover marked Israel's release from Egyptian slavery, so Christ's sacrificial death, which is the central theme of the Lord's Supper, marks our release from slavery to sin.

There were other feasts: Firstfruits, Pentecost, Trumpets, Atonement, and Tabernacles. However, these feasts foreshadowed the more mature aspects of our Christian life. Simply put, Passover was the feast of salvation. Therefore, Paul in writing this refers to our entry into the kingdom. He points out that Passover could not be celebrated with "the old bread of wickedness and evil." So the mindset of "he's a baby Christian" is faulty reasoning—for him and also for us. Often this is the rationale used to overlook a person who is "given to sin"; it's deceptive and misleading since there's no place for known, practiced sin in the church. (I'll discuss the difference between "known, practiced sin" and "falling into sin" in a later chapter.)

Second, notice Paul said this man's practice of sin is like yeast (or leaven). Yeast is a substance that spreads throughout the batch of dough and causes it to rise. Concerning the Feast of Passover, Israel was strongly warned, "On the first day of the festival, remove every trace of yeast from your homes. Anyone who eats bread made with yeast during the seven days of the festival will be *cut off* from the community of Israel" (Exodus 12:15). The words "cut off" are also decisive, no different than Paul's instruction. God did this to show both Israel and us that when we come into covenant with Him, there can be no one "given to sin" in the community. All must repent from known, practiced disobedience to His Word, or they will carry the yeast of sin and its consequences into their community.

The *Pillar New Testament Commentary* states:

> Paul emphasizes (by emphatic word order in Greek) that through
> only a "little" part of the church, one person in fact, the evil would
> inevitably, slowly but surely, spread through the whole community,
> if left unchecked. The example of willful sin in the church can have
> serious effects. Like leaven in bread, unchecked sin in the church
> spreads through the whole and irretrievably changes it.

I would disagree with one point this commentary makes. In research-
ing yeast, I've found it doesn't spread *slowly* but rather, *rapidly*. However,
what is undoubtedly true in this commentary is that it does spread *surely*
through the community.

Does this mean, then, that we should prevent anyone from coming
into our gatherings who is involved in practiced sin? Absolutely not!
There should be multitudes of unbelievers in our assemblies, but not as
members of the church, nor should they be made to *think they are members* unless they've repented of known, practiced sin and given their entire life to Jesus Christ. Paul makes this point clear:

> When I wrote to you before, I told you not to associate with people
> who indulge in sexual sin. But I wasn't talking about *unbelievers*
> who indulge in sexual sin, or are greedy, or cheat people, or wor-
> ship idols. You would have to leave this world to avoid people like
> that. (1 Corinthians 5:9–10)

We who follow Christ are commanded to go into the world, to reach
those in it, and to invite them to join us in our assemblies to hear the
Word of God—but not a compromised or limited version of the truth
about their spiritual condition. We are to continuously reach out, eat
with, befriend, love, and serve unbelievers, just as Jesus did.

However, Paul says something entirely different in regard to someone who confesses to be a believer:

> I meant that you are not to associate with *anyone who claims to be a believer* yet indulges in sexual sin, or is greedy, or worships idols, or is abusive, or is a drunkard, or cheats people. Don't even eat with such people. (1 Corinthians 5:11)

It is clear Paul is not speaking of a believer who "falls into sin" but rather one who considers himself a believer but is "given to sin." Why does this church father speak so strongly about this? Simply put, it is evidence of his true love for the church. He doesn't want to see the church at large suffer while *supposedly protecting* the "believer" who continues in sin.

Think of it this way: if someone has an extremely contagious disease—one that can be transmitted through the air to anyone nearby, what does the community do? They place the sick person in quarantine. This protects the larger community from catching the disease. If not, it will spread like wildfire, and the entire community will suffer from the disease and its consequences. What could be widespread consequences? Vacated positions, loss of productivity, an interruption of services to the community, and economic suffering—to name just a few.

Paul then states of this person who is given to sin:

> Then you must throw this man out and hand him over to Satan so that his sinful nature will be destroyed and he himself will be saved on the day the Lord returns. (1 Corinthians 5:5)

This brother is in grave danger of being lost forever if he doesn't change. This is why I used the words "supposedly protecting" previously. The truth of the matter is that the one in willful sin is in greater danger if allowed to remain in the community, for she or he will assume right standing with God and discover their lost state when it's too late on the day of judgment.

The hardships this person will face outside of God's protection will most likely cause him to come to his senses and return to Jesus with all of his heart and soul, which is exactly what happened with this man (described in Paul's second letter to the Corinthians). Hardships have a way of waking us up, such as in the case of the prodigal son. He returned home when he saw the fruit of his sinning ways. If his dad would have approved of him and kept sending money, the son wouldn't have come to the realization of his state of rebellion.

As It Is in Heaven . . .

Let's return to the main point. We have clearly seen in the past two chapters that we are one body of Christ, and as a body we can all benefit from an individual's contributions or suffer from a member's known and practiced sin.

There is truth here that can't be ignored. The effects of avoiding this discussion have sadly lingered on for too long in the body of Christ. These consequences won't go away if we continue to ignore these issues.

Let's be brave and confront them head-on. All heaven is cheering us on! We are called to be the triumphant church, the body of Christ that—no different than Jesus—is unstoppable. Sickness, disease, poverty, lack of resources, and the rest of the enemy's works should bow to the Lord's church.

We are called to reign in authority and be full of supernatural power to put heaven's enemies under our feet. And this we will do if we are not afraid to confront difficult issues that have plagued us.

We must dare to believe that it can be done on earth as it is in heaven!

TAKE ACTION

This issue is so important, and unfortunately it is rare to find a modern church that rightly emphasizes these truths. Consider this: First, God calls you to live free from sin, entirely given to Him. Second, when believers fail to do this, they not only affect their own lives but also the entire body of Christ.

Take time to reflect on all this. Don't let these truths be just good ideas and simply move along. Sit on them. Meditate on them. Pray through these truths and ask God about them for yourself. Let them really sink in and become as important to you as they were to Paul.

5

BE THE CHANGE

I'm one of many in my generation who have been taught more about our individual walk with Jesus than about how all of us believers are one body. Only recently has the reality of this truth about the church become more clear to me. I don't want to mislead you—I've certainly understood this truth in part in the past, but not to the extent I do now.

As the Holy Spirit has awakened my awareness to this reality, I've often thought of the Naval Sea, Air, and Land teams, commonly known as the Navy SEALs.

I have a friend who is a member of these elite warriors. He has been with SEAL teams for fifteen years and is currently an instructor. After pondering these truths about the body of Christ for some time, I decided to contact him. I knew SEALs were a close band of brothers, so I wanted to probe deeper. I called him and my first questions were, "How do SEALs view and interact with each other? How do they produce such a tight-knit community? And what is entailed in their training?"

His first comment to me, "The last person a SEAL thinks of is himself."

I loved how clear and concise he was right out of the gate. I knew it would be a revealing phone call and remained silent and let him continue.

"We value our brother next to us more than our self. We never have to cover our backs, because we know our SEAL brothers will."

At that point he started "preaching" to me: "If you look at the sixth chapter of Ephesians, you'll find the armor of God is all forward facing—nothing covers our rear side. The reason is that God intends for each of us to do what the SEALs do, to cover each other's backs—to think as one unit, one body. If we don't operate this way, I have only one person covering my back: me. However, if we all function as a team, I have every guy in my platoon covering my back."

He continued, "As a Navy SEAL, everything I do is for the sake of my brother next to me. We believe this to the very core of our being. We are trained not to think of ourselves as individuals, but as a unit. Even though we are trained as experts in different areas—explosives, communications, sniper, medic, JTAC, weapons, breaching, and so on, we function as one unit. We never go on a mission with the mentality of, *Some of us may not come back*, or *only forty percent of us will make it back*. No, our attitude is, *One hundred percent of us go in and one hundred percent of us come back*."

I was captivated by what he was revealing. Eventually, I asked, "How do you train this attitude into your recruits?"

"You can't!" he replied. "The Basic Underwater Demolition/SEAL training training is considered the most arduous, difficult training in the military and is why approximately ninety percent of those who sign up for the SEAL program either quit or get washed out. What remains is a unit of highly trained, fully equipped individuals. Each one values the man next to him more than himself and is willing to die for a cause bigger than himself."

He then said, "John, if only the church would behave this way. What would happen?"

Sadly, I could only agree. However, the truth is that we do have the potential for this. It is a very real part of the *divine nature* placed in us when we are born again. The preaching and teaching we receive, which is *our* training, should locate this attitude and flesh it out. But if we only hear a consumer version of the gospel, we will develop the wrong thing— our unredeemed flesh. This is largely why the modern church is in the shape we are in. Many of us only want to be encouraged and uplifted, rather than challenged. We're missing so much.

My friend is a warrior, yet he perceived the weakness of the church in modern times. He knew that if one member of a SEAL platoon was weak, compromised, or had abandoned his post, all the team members would suffer as a group or die because of that one person's laziness or incompetence. What is ingrained in him is what we need embedded in our psyche as members of the body of Christ.

Be the Change

Is there a positive aspect of what we've been discussing? Absolutely—with God there always is!

I realize you could view the truths from previous chapters negatively and grow discouraged and disillusioned. If you dwell only on the reality of how the actions of others could possibly adversely affect your life, yes, it can be disheartening. However, the reason for bringing this truth to light is to see us progress corporately and see the full measure of His greatness and power like we've not seen in our generation. There will be no change if we don't believe or do anything different. So here's the bottom line: *You can be the change.* If it doesn't begin with you or me, how can it begin? God has called us to be agents of change!

Have you ever observed what happens when a person who has a tender conscience but is a bit unruly outwardly, suddenly takes on the responsibility of other's lives? Often this brings out the best in that individual! For example, think of a young mother. She was sometimes wild, crazy, and even a little stupid when she was single. Her actions only affected her own life and no one else. But then she falls in love, marries, and has a child. Now this once somewhat out-of-control girl straightens up. If she continues to be foolish, rowdy, and live dangerously, she knows it will not just affect her life but also the lives of the husband and child she loves.

This is what must happen with each of us in regard to the church. We must love each other deeply. We must realize there's a sure possibility we're not the only ones affected by disobeying God's Word. We are part of a body! Perhaps this is why Paul writes this command in the midst of discussing the Lord's Supper to the Corinthian church:

You say, "I am allowed to do anything"—but not everything is beneficial. Don't be concerned for your own good but for the good of others. (1 Corinthians 10:23–24)

And again Paul tells the Philippian church:

Let each regard the others as better than *and* superior to himself [thinking more highly of one another than you do of yourselves]. . . . Let this same attitude *and* purpose *and* [humble] mind be in you which was in Christ Jesus. (Philippians 2:3, 5 AMPC)

This is the mindset Jesus had, the heart of what motivated Him to come and give His life for us. He could have saved Himself. He could have called for a legion of angels to deliver Him from the hands of His executioners, but He had us on His mind. He cared more about our well-being than His own.

Here is the good news: When we as individuals walk in obedience to God's Word, ultimately we will be blessed. We may go through uncomfortable and even difficult times due to the disobedience of some in the body, but we will ultimately prosper.

Elijah is an example of such suffering from others' behavior. Due to Ahab and Jezebel's continuous sin, as well as the people of Israel's indifference to sin, there was no rain on the earth for years. Elijah wasn't eating bountifully, as the people had eaten in the days of King David and King Solomon's reigns. Instead he had to eat bread and meat brought to him by ravens for years—that wasn't cool! It was a monotonous diet with no vegetables, honey, juice, or the many other delicacies available in abundant times. This was a hardship for him because of the actions of others. But Elijah was a part of one nation, one people, and one body. His obedience eventually brought change and . . . rain. This blessed the nation and in the end, he was personally blessed.

Covenant of Peace

If we look at another incident before Elijah's time, again we see *many* suffering from the actions of *some*. Israel was in the desert, camped at Acacia Grove. We read:

> *Some* of the men defiled themselves by having sexual relations with
> local Moabite women. These women invited them to attend sac-
> rifices to their gods, so the Israelites feasted with them and wor-
> shiped the gods of Moab. In this way, Israel joined in the worship
> of Baal of Peor, causing the Lord's anger to blaze against his people.
> (Numbers 25:1–3)

Again, notice the word "some." God had told His people to not worship other gods, give themselves to foreign women, or commit sexual immorality. But the disobedient actions of *some* brought judgment to the entire congregation (nation), and we will see again not *some*, but *many*, were affected by this judgment.

> The LORD issued the following command to Moses: "Seize all the
> ringleaders and execute them before the Lord in broad daylight,

so His fierce anger will turn away from the people of Israel."
(Numbers 25:4)

Again, we discover the actions of the ringleaders (*some*) caused the fierce jealous anger of the Lord to burn against all of Israel. They were one nation, one people, and one body.

About the same time Moses issued the command to execute the ringleaders, a particular Israelite man named Simeon took a Midianite woman named Cozbi into his tent in front of Moses and all the people. This was known and unacceptable disobedience to the Word of the Lord. Immediately, Phinehas, the son of Eleazar and the grandson of Aaron, grabbed a spear and ran into Simeon's tent and thrust the spear through not only Simeon, but also Cozbi, executing both of them with one jab. We then read, "So the plague against the Israelites was stopped, but not before 24,000 people had died" (Numbers 25:8–9). Once again, many died; many suffered; many were affected by the actions of *some*. The nation was *one* in God's eyes.

God then declares, "'Phinehas the son of Eleazar, the son of Aaron the priest, has turned back My wrath from the children of Israel, because he was zealous with My zeal among them, so that I did not consume the children of Israel in My zeal'" (Numbers 25:10–11 NKJV). Phinehas's passion was God's passion—the good of the entire nation. Phinehas was the one who brought the change for better. It didn't take everyone, just one man.

Paul was the one man who was passionate with God's passion for the church at Corinth. He was the one who brought the change by boldly confronting the church with truth. He took the Word of God—the Sword of the Spirit—and thrust it through the activity of the one man living in sexual immorality. In the Old Testament, it was a physical spear; in the New Testament and today, the "spear" comes out when we boldly stand up and speak the truth, even when others are turning a deaf ear or a blind eye to the known sin of one or some in a community.

The last person Paul was thinking about was himself. He was acting no different than my Navy SEAL friend. He put the good of others before his own comfort and popularity. He even risked total rejection by the church of Corinth. He was zealous for them, even when it turned out that the more he loved them, the less they loved him.

Phinehas didn't care about himself; he knew he could have been accused of being harsh, cruel, unsympathetic, backward, extreme in his belief, or old-fashioned. He was one man and no one else was moving. What would people think, say, or do? None of this mattered. The psalmist states, "Phinehas had the courage to intervene" (Psalm 106:30). He was zealous for God and for what God cared for—His people. He loved the community. He was the agent of change!

Now look at what God says about him:

"Therefore say, 'Behold, I give to him *My covenant of peace*; and it shall be to *him* and *his descendants* after him a covenant of an everlasting priesthood, because he was zealous for his God, and made atonement for the children of Israel.'" (Numbers 25:12–13 NKJV)

This statement has stood out to me over the many years of my Bible study. Not only did Moses write about it, but also the psalmist much later emphasized his reward:

Then Phinehas stood up and intervened, and the plague was stopped. And that was accounted to him for righteousness to all generations forevermore. (Psalm 106:30–31 NKJV)

I remember the awe I felt when I first saw the great reward for this young man who took the risk of standing up for what pleased God. Not just a temporary reward, but an eternal reward, one sealed with a covenant. Remember, God never breaks His covenants. This reward is so great it wouldn't just affect him, but all his children and children's children to all generations after them—*including ours*! All subsequent generations would be rewarded for his willingness to stand up for what was right in the eyes of God.

When I saw this example of Phinehas, I purposed that I would always speak the truth, even if the result would be a loss of love like what Paul experienced. I could see the great reward for not only me, but for Lisa and our sons and their children for all generations to come. It would be a covenant of peace, one that can never be broken, a blessing that would endure from generation to generation.

Thus, it's been overwhelming to me to see how passionately our sons serve God. I was away from home ministering the gospel for at least half the days every year when they were growing up. Yet, it seems the covenant of peace God promises to those who will be the agents of change was secured and protected for our children. I expect the same blessing for our grandchildren as well.

Is there a blessing hidden in heeding the truths we've uncovered so far? Yes, it is the *covenant of peace* that is promised not only to you, but also to your descendants, as long as you are the voice of change—as long as you are zealous for God's ways, even when others are not.

Are we seeing together how it is better to speak out using the sword of the spirit in love than to remain silent and watch sin prevail and spread through our community of believers?

To me the answer is obvious, but I'll leave your determination to you.

TAKE ACTION

Here is the good news you've been waiting for: Taking a firm stance for truth, when done in love for God and His people, puts you in company with people who received eternal, covenant promises of blessing from

God that determined the future not just for their lives, but for their descendants too.

Can you think of anything else more powerful you could do for your posterity? No worldly, physical inheritance carries that promise—money could be squandered in a generation or two. No amount of knowledge or wisdom amassed could possibly pass down to that many generations. Only an inheritance based on a promise of God's faithfulness could have such a long-lasting impact.

What legacy do you want to leave to future generations? How do you want to be remembered on earth, and how do you want to be known in heaven? The greatest key to these desires coming to pass is how firmly you will stand for love and truth during your short years on earth.

6

THE MOTIVATION

Recently, I experienced difficulty in sending texts on my iPhone. I tried everything to fix the problem, from closing apps, to shutting off my phone and rebooting, all the way to the "force quit": the action you turn to when nothing else seems to work. I then proceeded to more complicated steps, but there was no relief from the annoying problem.

This experience confirmed how much we rely on and how important our smartphones are in everyday life. It just so happened that our youngest son was in India speaking at a conference and distributing books to pastors and leaders. He ran into some difficulties and was texting me, but I couldn't reply to his messages for hours due to the glitch in my phone. It took more than fifteen minutes to type out a sentence or two, then my phone would suddenly back out of the app, losing everything typed, and I'd have to start the process all over. I got one short text to him in four hours. I wanted to say more, but couldn't. Needless to say, I was very frustrated.

Finally, I brought my phone to experts—technicians who knew far more about how it worked. I'd attempted to solve the problem for days, but they got to the root of the trouble in less than fifteen minutes. Within a couple of hours, I was texting once again without any problems. Turns out I had inadvertently done something that jammed up the phone's operating system.

What if I hadn't sought out the solution? What if I hadn't taken the time to consult the experts? I would still be using the phone far beneath its intended functioning level and, tragically, wasting a lot of time. It would have hindered communicating with my family, team, and friends.

Let's take it a step further. Suppose I'd never experienced the reality of texting? Thirty years ago, I didn't even know what a text was, let alone a smartphone. Just a hundred years ago, there wasn't even a transcontinental phone call; it didn't exist. Back then, I would have been delighted to labor four hours just to send an instant message to my son in India. Any communication would have been better than no communication at all.

Without knowing what was available to me, I wouldn't have been so diligent to seek out the solution and press through the difficulties standing in my way. But with my iPhone, I had experienced the benefits, so it was this knowledge that caused the frustration level to be so high.

Without knowing our potential, there will be an absence of the desire and drive to achieve something. Most of us don't know the power of a united military unit, as my friend the Navy SEAL does. Can you imagine if he had a glitch in his platoon that was causing failure? He wouldn't just be irritated . . . but quite possibly dead.

Thinking back to the Old Testament story, can you imagine the exasperation level of Israel with Achan? They had experienced great success in the battle of Jericho, but after Ai were attending thirty-six funerals of close friends and consoling the families of dead soldiers.

Can you imagine Paul's frustration in seeing his beloved Corinthians suffer the terrible consequences of spiritual kryptonite—weakness, unshakable sickness, and premature death? He was well aware of their potential, but they were blind to it. Their personal preferences outweighed the greater good of the community.

What about you? And what about the Christian community you're a part of? I would imagine that the reason you are reading this challenging message is because you know deep down there's *more* to the Christian experience. God has placed this desire in your heart. You're more interested in living a full life in His presence and witnessing dynamic spiritual transformation in your community than avoiding the temporary discomfort of truth.

Your Light Has Come

There are two major benefits that will result from our study in this book: One will significantly heighten your community's effectiveness, and the other will enhance you personally with greater fruitfulness, fulfillment, and intimacy with God. (Up to this point our focus has been on community, but eventually we'll transition our focus back to you as an individual.)

What should our vision be for our community? As with the example of my iPhone, the answer to this question will fuel the desire and motivation to continue searching out and rectifying what hinders us from our potential.

Isaiah prophesies:

> Arise, shine; for your light has come!
> And the glory of the Lord is risen upon you.
> For behold, the darkness shall cover the earth, and deep darkness
> the people; but the Lord will arise over you, and His glory will be
> seen upon you. (Isaiah 60:1–2 NKJV)

The first thing I want to point out is that Isaiah is not referring to heaven. And he's also not speaking of the millennial reign of Christ—the time period when Jesus will reign on this earth for a thousand years, as depicted in the book of Revelation. The prophet is also not referring to the new heaven and earth that Peter and other writers foretell. No, he is describing the time period when darkness shall cover the earth. So this prophecy certainly can, and I believe is, speaking of our day.

According to the prophet, deep darkness is going to be upon the people, not just in geographic pockets, but the entire earth. We are living in a time when darkness is growing deeper. We are drifting further and further from the heart of our Creator. I'm not speaking only of atheists, agnostics, and those in cults, but many who profess Christianity. This is the time when Paul specifically states, "People will no longer listen to sound and wholesome teaching. They will follow their own desires and will look for teachers who will tell them whatever their itching ears want to hear" (2 Timothy 4:3). He then laments, "They will turn their ears away from the truth" (verse 4 NKJV).

In this time period, Isaiah states that authentic believers are going to shine—stand out. Think of it like this: If you walk into a dark room and flip on the light switch, darkness is immediately expelled. Darkness can't overcome light; have you ever heard of a flash-dark? No, only a flashlight, because no matter how dark it is, light overcomes and expels darkness.

Jesus states we are the light of the world. We should shine, we should be stronger than darkness, but how and what does this look like? According to Isaiah, we should shine in a way that unbelievers will see His *glory.*

The Hebrew word for "glory" is *kabod,* which means splendor, greatness, wealth, might, abundance, honor, majesty, and heaviness. Think for a moment of what is being stated. When the Bible speaks of the glory of God, it's referring to the splendor of God, the greatness of God, the wealth of God, the might of God, the abundance of God, the honor of God, and the majesty of God. The final definitive word "heaviness" or "weight" would indicate these attributes are not in short supply, but rather at full strength. Simply put, it's the weight of His greatness.

Paul writes that God has placed this knowledge "in our hearts so we could know the glory of God" (2 Corinthians 4:6). He goes on to say:

We now have this light shining in our hearts, but we ourselves are like fragile clay jars containing this great treasure. This makes

it clear that *our great power* is from God, not from ourselves.
(2 Corinthians 4:7)

Notice his words, "our great power." The splendor, greatness, wealth, abundance, honor, and majesty of God shine in our hearts in full strength. This is why he states, "*our great power* is from God, not from ourselves." We are talking power here—the power to pierce through any darkness that would try to stand in the way of our mission.

When a Navy SEAL platoon goes out on a mission, they don't plan on coming back defeated, and they usually don't. We have a more sure promise than a Navy SEAL! And it's backed by much greater power to succeed!

To help keep the meaning consistently clear for the rest of this book, I'll frequently refer to "His glory" as "His greatness" (but keep in mind the other defining words I've listed in the above paragraphs).

Isaiah states that the reality of His greatness will *arise* upon us, not *descend upon* us. Arise from where? From our hearts! Remember, "we have this treasure in earthen vessels" (verse 7 NKJV).

So I ask, "Why isn't His magnificent greatness being revealed through us to our society? Why are so many weak, sick, and even dying prematurely? Is it due to our tolerating spiritual kryptonite?"

The Potential of Community

Just what could be the positive potential of community today? Consider the beginning of the church. On the day of Pentecost, the disciples, who numbered about 120, were hiding in a room. We are told they were of "one accord." What facilitated this unity? When Jesus rose from the dead, He told at least five hundred believers to go to the upper room and wait for the promise of the Father (see 1 Corinthians 15:6 and Luke 24:33–53). Why were there only 120 just ten days later? Why weren't they all waiting, and what happened to the other 380? There is no mention of them again, only that some were still alive in the year AD 56, the time Paul wrote the letter to the Corinthians. What we do know for sure is that they didn't wait for the promise of the Father in Jerusalem, which Jesus had commanded (see Acts 1:1–15).

Could these 380 have viewed His directive as optional, merely a good suggestion? Or possibly did they think it was too difficult to fulfill this request? Perhaps they believed they could serve Him as they saw fit. I'm sure some were even out preaching the resurrection.

However, the Spirit of God, who is also referred to as the Spirit of *glory* (see 1 Peter 4:14), didn't fill them. It was the 120 who were one who were baptized with the Spirit of God's greatness. What made them one? It wasn't that they held to their own opinions, which may describe the 380. I believe it was their resolute obedience to the Word of God, which they didn't see as optional.

God's glory (which includes His power) filled them and that very day, over three thousand were born again! They didn't hand out flyers, advertise in Jewish magazines, employ mass social media strategies, or blitz the airwaves with advertisements. In fact, no meeting was scheduled. Yet God's greatness was revealed to the entire city.

A short time later, another five thousand men, not counting women and children, were born again after a man who was born crippled jumped up and ran into the temple. The startling reality with this multitude being converted is that Peter and John didn't even have time to give an invitation for salvation—they were arrested before they could!

The entire city of Jerusalem was in an uproar over what was taking place. They all heard the sound of a mighty wind. The city's residents heard the disciples speak wonderful declarations of God's greatness in foreign languages and dialects that they had never before studied. Everyone saw notable miracles being done in the name of Jesus.

A few days later, they all prayed as a community and the entire building where they were assembled shook. The Bible doesn't exaggerate. If it states the building shook, you can bet it rocked. There was great power, abundance, and healing flowing from these believers.

The report was, "There were no needy people among them" (Acts 4:34). We see Peter walking the streets, not a singular street, but *streets* and all the sick and diseased who were laid on these streets just had to get within a shadow's distance of him, and Scripture reports, "They were all healed" (Acts 5:16). That's God's greatness! This would be like a believer walking through the halls of a hospital and healing every sick person.

The Scripture also tells us that a man and his wife acted irreverently by lying to the pastor in one of their services and fell over dead. The report of these deaths spread throughout the city and caused "great fear" to come upon everyone who heard, but the people esteemed the disciples highly (see Acts 5:1–13). This healthy fear didn't drive people away; rather, large numbers came: "Yet more and more people believed and were brought to the Lord—crowds of both men and women" (Acts 5:14).

This wasn't limited to Jerusalem. The followers of Jesus were witnessing boldly and entire cities were getting saved and healed. Philip, a man who bused tables for widows in a restaurant, went to a city in Samaria. We are told, "Many evil spirits were cast out, screaming as they left their victims. And many who had been paralyzed or lame were healed. So there was great joy in that city" (Acts 8:7–8). A well-known sorcerer was "amazed by the signs and great miracles Philip performed" (verse 13). The entire city either knew about or came to Jesus for salvation.

We read in another incident that Peter instantly healed a paralyzed man who had been bedridden for eight years. Scripture records that after this "the whole population of Lydda and Sharon saw Aeneas walking around, and they turned to the Lord" (Acts 9:35). Not just one city, but two cities, and we are specifically told the "whole population" was saved.

In Joppa, a lady named Tabitha was raised from the dead, and the news spread through the entire town—yet another locale is impacted in its entirety.

Peter is eventually arrested, but an angel comes into this maximum-security prison and breaks him out in the middle of the night.

A ruler is struck dead and eaten by worms for not giving God glory. God's greatness is exposing the darkness in the entire nation. There's just no escaping the light!

The miracles, great power, and individuals saved start spreading to the Gentile communities and cities. In fact, we are told at one point that "all who dwelt in Asia heard the word of the Lord Jesus, both Jews and Greeks" (Acts 19:10 NKJV). This is not only a few towns or even some cities, but an entire region. And *all* heard! They had no social media like Facebook, Instagram, or Twitter. There weren't any web pages, satellite communications, television, or radio. There were no automobiles or even bicycles so people could easily assemble! Yet everyone in this entire region heard the word of the Lord! This is what happens when the church becomes one—when God's Word takes preeminence in our Christian communities.

This is the divine greatness that manifested among the early church. However, in the next chapter we will see that God's plan for our generation is even greater. What they experienced in the early church is not even close to the divine greatness and power that will usher in the return of our Lord and King, Jesus Christ!

TAKE ACTION

When we see the incredible miracles of the New Testament, it can be easy to think, *Well, that was great for them, but someone like me could never do those kinds of things.* That's why the message of this chapter is so important—the signs and wonders didn't happen because the people were anyone special. They happened because these common people simply believed and obeyed, resulting in God's greatness rising up within them.

If God's greatness can rise up in them—loudmouthed, uneducated, young, inexperienced, opinionated people who worked mundane, ordinary jobs—then we can know there is no worldly standard that qualifies us to carry heavenly greatness. It's just a question of how faithfully we will believe and follow God's Word.

Do you believe it's possible to see these miracles again, and even more? If your church started seeing these things happen, would you jump in with both feet? Do you want to receive all God wants to give you? Express these answers as a prayer to God. Then repent for any way you have considered yourself unqualified or disqualified for this life. Give your concerns to God, and offer yourself to Him for all He has for you.

7

THE POWER
OF ONE

Jesus, before being crucified, had the opportunity to pray a final time for not only His team, but for all of us. He prefaces His request with, "'I am praying not only for these disciples but also for all who will ever believe in Me through their message'" (John 17:20). There's no denying He was including you and me. We came to know Jesus through their messages, either directly by reading them or indirectly by someone telling us what these disciples wrote.

Jesus is the Son of man; therefore, He has the authority to ask for the Father's will to be done on earth as it is in heaven. Hear what He prays:

> I pray that they will all be *one*, just as You and I are *one*—as You
> are in Me, Father, and I am in You. And may they be in us so that
> the world will believe You sent Me. I have given them the *glory* You
> gave Me, so they may be *one* as We are *one*. (John 17:21–22)

His prayer is that we would be *one*, so the world would believe that Jesus Christ is the Savior of all humankind. What will carry this message to our world? The answer is none other than His *glory*. This is crucial to our mission. He has reserved His glory (His revealed greatness) for those who are *one*, but here is the key: *being one in Him as He is one with the Father.*

How was He one with the Father? He repeatedly makes statements such as, "'I carry out the will of the one who sent Me, not My own will'" (John 5:30). And again, "'I have come down from heaven to do the will of God who sent Me, not to do My own will'" (John 6:38). And, "'I'm here to do it Your way, O God, the way it's described in Your Book'" (Hebrews 10:7 MSG). He was one with the Father because He sought out and did what His Father desired, even when it was not popular or comfortable.

The same was true for the first disciples. They were all in *one accord* on the day God revealed His greatness through them to the known world. It was the 120 followers, not the tens of thousands who had listened to Jesus over His three years of ministry. It was not the 380 who saw Him in His resurrected body, yet viewed His words as optional. It was those who were united in faith.

Paul pleads, even begs all of us: "Make every effort to keep yourselves united in the Spirit" (Ephesians 4:3). He then tells of the giftings Jesus has personally given the church—the apostles, prophets, evangelists, pastors, and teachers. Their responsibility is to build up the church with a targeted mission:

> This will continue until we all come to such *unity* in our faith
> and knowledge of God's Son that we will be mature in the Lord,
> measuring up to the full and complete standard of Christ.
> (Ephesians 4:13)

Our mission or goal is no different than that of the early church: to be *one* and subsequently become a revealer of God's greatness (glory). There is no other way! Our generation must become one—unified in our faith and knowledge. The only path to true oneness is no different than that of Jesus or the disciples: obedience to the Word of God.

Think of it: When Israel was one, they soundly defeated Jericho. When Israel was one under Solomon's reign, they were invincible as a nation and individuals were living successful and satisfied lives in a way few generations have experienced. There are other examples, too, but the point is clear.

On the other hand, look at the opposite. When Paul addressed the spiritual kryptonite in Corinth, he starts out his message with, "First, I hear that there are divisions among you when you meet as a church" (1 Corinthians 11:18). Obviously, they were not *one*! The question arises: What prevented them from being one? It was their flirtation with kryptonite—their disobedience to God's Word. This was no different than how Achan's disobedience to God's Word caused Israel to no longer be one and invincible when they attacked Ai.

Paul then turns it around and makes a statement that sounds counterintuitive:

> . . . And to some extent I believe it. But, of course, there must be divisions among you so that you who have God's approval will be recognized! (1 Corinthians 11:18–19)

Why is it important for those who have God's approval to be recognized? The answer is important in paving the way to oneness in faith and knowledge. This is just as important as it was for the majority's obedience and Achan's disobedience to be revealed for the sake of the entire community of Israel and their mission. Just as it was important for 120 unwavering, obedient disciples to be segregated from the 380 who did it their own way, in the same way, it was important for the church in Corinth. The obedient *majority* and the disobedient *some* needed to stand out; if not, the road to unity would be blocked and thereby hold back God's glory (greatness) from being revealed in Corinth. It was also important to bring a remedy to the innocent bystanders who weren't irreverent toward the

Lord's Supper, but who were personally suffering (those weak, sick, and dying prematurely) because some were disrespectful.

Paul was well aware of the importance of making unity a priority. He knew what had happened in Jerusalem, Samaria, Antioch, and other cities that were completely and thoroughly impacted by God's greatness. This is why he not only begged for oneness in the Corinthian church, but also urged the same for the believers in Ephesus, Philippi, and Colossae— as well as all of us today to be one. From Jesus's example, we know there is no other avenue to this oneness than obedience to the Word of God.

Greater

So what about today? Is unity of the faith still the goal? Let me start by sharing an experience in prayer I'll never forget. I heard so clearly, "Son, the book of Acts will seem like child's play in comparison to what I'm about to do in and through the church prior to My Son's return."

I was in shock. In fact, I didn't believe what I had heard. I countered by saying, "Father, I need three different references from the Bible to believe this." Interestingly, I sensed no displeasure in asking for this. We are to *test all things* (see 1 Thessalonians 5:21) and are told, "'By the mouth of two or three witnesses every word shall be established'" (2 Corinthians 13:1 NKJV).

One of the references He directed me to is:

"For thus says the Lord of hosts: 'Once more (it *is* a little while) I will shake heaven and earth, the sea and dry land; and I will shake all nations, and they shall come to the Desire of All Nations, and I will fill this temple with glory,' says the Lord of hosts. 'The glory of this latter temple shall be greater than the former,' says the Lord of hosts." (Haggai 2:6–7, 9 NKJV)

A little history: Israel had been in captivity for many years, initially to the Babylonians and then to the Persians. God had put it in the heart of King Cyrus of Persia to release the Hebrews who desired to return to their homeland and rebuild the temple Nebuchadnezzar and his Babylonian army had destroyed. Many returned to their homeland and started reconstruction enthusiastically, but then eventually lost interest due to the combination of personal interests with the nagging resistance from the locals. It took the prophesying of Haggai, Zechariah, and other leaders to rekindle the desire to unite in rebuilding God's house.

However, the crucial question is: Was the prophet referring to the temple they'd eventually finish, or to another temple? Later Jesus said He would "'destroy this temple, and in three days I will raise it up'" (John 2:19). Even though He was standing in the middle of the physical temple, He wasn't referring to it, but rather the temple of His body. Is this the case here?

Bible commentaries and historians report that the physical temple that was rebuilt after Israel's seventy-year captivity didn't surpass the greatness of Solomon's, both in appearance as well as in God's manifest presence. In regard to appearance, even hundreds of years later after Herod embellished the building, it still is not believed to be more glorious than Solomon's original. In regard to presence, when Solomon dedicated the physical temple, the glory of God was so great a thick cloud filled the building and the priests couldn't continue their service. History doesn't show anything as dramatic as this happening in the restored temple.

The Pharisees misunderstood Jesus's statement about destroying the temple and rebuilding it in three days, because they assumed it was the physical temple. Even so, if we limit Haggai's statement to the physical temple, we will also misunderstand the meaning.

What temple is he referring to, and what is the time period? Paul states, "Don't you realize that *all of you together* are the temple of God and that the Spirit of God lives in you?" (1 Corinthians 3:16). The same Spirit that filled Solomon's temple lives fully in us—collectively. I believe this is the temple Haggai speaks of, and the church is the latter temple; its glory (greatness of God's presence and power) is greater than the former physical temple. Paul writes, "If that law which disappeared came with glory, then this new way . . . has much greater glory" (2 Corinthians 3:11 NCV).

Think about the glory (greatness and power) revealed in the Old Testament: Moses's face so shines with God's great splendor that a veil has to be put over his face to dim it. Once the tabernacle is built, God's presence manifests so powerfully that no one can come near. Once Solomon builds and dedicates the temple, the revealed presence of God once again is so awesome the priests can't continue their service. His glorious presence was something amazing—awesome indeed, however, according to Paul "that first glory was not glorious at all compared with the overwhelming glory of the new way" (2 Corinthians 3:10).

But what about the time period—is Haggai discussing the church from beginning to end? In other words, is it from the time of Jesus's ascension to the time of His second coming?

Look again at God's words as written down by Haggai:

> "'Once more (it is a little while) I will shake heaven and earth, the
> sea and dry land; and I will shake all nations, and they shall come
> to the Desire of All Nations, and I will fill this temple with glory.'"
> (Haggai 2:6–7)

The glory He refers to occurs in the time period the shaking occurs. The writer of Hebrews confirms this: "He makes another promise: 'Once again I will shake not only the earth but the heavens also.' This means that all of creation will be shaken and removed, so that only unshakable things will remain" (Hebrews 12:26–27).

The book of Hebrews was written in AD 68, long after the events I cited in the previous chapter, i.e., sick people being laid on the streets of Jerusalem, cities coming to the Lord, entire regions hearing the Word of God, and so forth. Therefore, the promise in Hebrews is not referring to the time period of the book of Acts but rather to the future—the time period of the end when all of creation will be shaken. This has to be the latter generation that will see the return of the Lord Jesus Christ.

A well-established pattern is seen throughout Scripture: *God always saves the best for last.* We are told, "The end of a thing is better than its beginning" (Ecclesiastes 7:8 NKJV). Jesus displays this pattern by saving the best wine for last at the wedding of Cana. Later, He declares that "anyone who believes in me will do the same works I have done, and even *greater* works" (John 14:12). Why would the "greater" come after Jesus ascended into heaven? Because He always saves the best for last.

The same is true for the church; its end will be better than its beginning. The book of Acts shows a remarkable beginning, so can you possibly believe that the end of the church's time on earth will be less glorious, less powerful, less impactful than the beginning? Remember, Paul emphatically states, "Your faith should not be in the wisdom of men but in the power of God," and again that "the kingdom of God is not in word but in power" (1 Corinthians 2:5 and 4:20 NKJV). Power is a huge aspect of God's manifested kingdom on earth.

Restoration

There are more Scriptures the Holy Spirit led me to that day, but it's obvious from the few I've shared that our vision as believers needs to expand—in fact, even to exceed what we read in the book of Acts. It's interesting to note the apostle Peter, filled with the Holy Spirit, declares:

He will again send you Jesus, your appointed Messiah. For He must remain in heaven until the time for the final restoration of

all things, as God promised long ago through His holy prophets.
(Acts 3:20–21)

Let's look at these words closely. First, Jesus must remain in heaven until something happens. That means He cannot come back until what our Father has promised occurs. What is that promise, which also the prophets spoke about? It is the restoration of the temple. In other words, the splendor, greatness, wealth, abundance, honor, and majesty of God will no longer be in short supply on earth, but rather revealed at full strength in and through His temple.

Is this currently happening? Is the church so powerful that we are seeing entire cities or regions coming to salvation? Are we seeing hospitals emptied? Are we seeing blind eyes opened, people crippled from birth leaping, jumping, and praising God? Are buildings shaking from the power of our prayers? Are we seeing such abundance there is no short supply of resources among ministries and churches to reach the lost in any nation? Is there no need among individuals in the church? Could this be why the prophet Haggai asks:

> "Does anyone remember this house—this Temple—in its former splendor? How, in comparison, does it look to you now? It must seem like *nothing at all!*" (Haggai 2:3)

Haggai was asking this of the people standing before him, but just as much, God is asking this of us today. Let's be honest: In comparison to the book of Acts, His manifest presence we experience now seems like *nothing at all!* If we don't clearly see this, we will not passionately seek His great power to be restored to the church. Instead, we will settle for remaining a powerless church.

Can we afford to tolerate a lack of unity that is fostered by the kryptonite that plagues us? Please, please hear me—we must press on toward the goal of being one in Him, and that can only occur through belief and obedience to His Word.

Now that the vision of where we must go is clear, let's return to identifying the kryptonite that is hindering our progress, both individually and as a community of believers.

TAKE ACTION

Until we know what is possible, we cannot be discontent with the little we have accepted as normal. But now, having read this chapter, you know what is possible, so you face a clear decision: Accept the weak and powerless life of limited influence much of the church has known, or embrace a lifelong pursuit of a powerful life that displays the full, raw greatness of Jesus Christ.

Until you have confidence in this possibility, you cannot take action. Without action, you will live in relative powerlessness by default. This means that the first step toward action is to choose to take confidence in God's Word and His vision for your life.

Ephesians tells us Jesus washes us clean with His words, and we can use our words to partner with Him in this process. Write declarations about the powerful life you are called to—statements like, "Jesus has filled me with His Spirit of power to change my world," or, "God causes His greatness to rise up from within me to reach the lost," or, "I am anointed to influence my peers and transform my workplace"—and begin declaring these truths over yourself every day. Then watch as your confidence to take action grows steadily day by day.

IDENTIFYING KRYPTONITE

SECTION 2

8

A MARRIAGE COVENANT

It may seem for the next few chapters that we are going on a rabbit trail, but I assure you that after we establish a few important truths, we will continue to address the spiritual kryptonite that plagues the church.

A Typical Marriage?

Consider this story, which I believe illustrates the sacred exclusivity of our relationship with God better than any other example I can think of.

A young man named Justin has been dating Angela for a year. She's beautiful in his eyes and possesses a magnificent personality. He's deeply in love with her and knows she's the one he wants to spend the rest of his life with.

Justin plans the special evening. At the perfect moment, he gets on one knee and opens the tiny box to present her with a magnificent diamond engagement ring.

Angela's completely overwhelmed. In shock, she covers her face and her tears of joy begin to flow. Overcome with emotion, she silently but passionately nods her head. When a little more composed, she lets out a cheerful, "Yes, yes, yes, I'll marry you!"

The storybook wedding takes place a few months later. The honeymoon that follows is full of love, laughs, adventures, and dreaming together of their future. It's everything a young man and woman could have wished for, and more.

Time passes, and Justin happily discovers that Angela is more amazing than he had thought. She likes adventure, loves having fun, and has a great sense of humor. She's great with his family and gets along with most everyone. She's smart, witty, and always seems to be one step ahead of him. She's creative, artistic, and imaginative. Justin's awed by the beautiful touches she consistently adds to their home. She's a better chef than him and as a wonderful bonus, she's neat and organized. Needless to say, he's enjoying her contribution to their newly formed union. Their future looks very bright.

A few months into their marriage, once they've settled into the rhythm of married life, one evening Justin returns home from work. He anticipates finding Angela waiting for what's become the traditional embrace and kiss. He searches for her—first the family room, then the kitchen, the back yard and finally the bedroom, where he finally finds her.

It appears she's preparing to go out. Romantic music fills the room, along with what has become the familiar scent of her perfume. To Justin's surprise she's all made up and slipping into a beautiful outfit, one that she had worn in the past when he took her to a favorite restaurant.

Her back faces him so she hasn't seen her husband walk in the room yet. Justin panics: *Oh no, did we have dinner plans for tonight that I forgot about? I should have stopped by the florist and gotten her a bouquet of roses!*

He breaks the silence with a cheerful but nervous greeting, "Hey, honey."

A little startled, she happily responds, "Oh, hey babe."

He opens with a confession, "Okay, I guess I've forgotten something. Did we have plans tonight?"

She immediately replies, "Oh no, baby."

is saying goodbye to an intimate relationship with every other man on the face of the earth. She is terminating all past relationships with any boyfriends, as well as declaring there will not be any new relationships with any other lovers from this day forward. And the man waiting for her at the front of the aisle is saying the same thing.

So let's make it personal. How would you react if you ran into a situation similar to what Justin faced? Or what if the one you were planning to marry told you beforehand, during your engagement period, this would be their behavior once united to you? Would you still go through with the ceremony?

I don't think so. You'd blurt out, *"No way!"*

Why would you be so adamant in your response? The simple answer is that you would not want to enter into a covenant on different terms. You'd resist pledging your entire life to the relationship while your spouse was not fully committed.

So you would never marry anyone under this condition or overlook this unacceptable behavior once married. Let's be honest and ask, "Can we actually believe Jesus is coming back for a bride who is acting like Angela?" Pause for a moment and think about it. Our relationship with Him is compared to a husband and wife. Paul says:

> As the Scriptures say, "A man leaves his father and mother and is joined to his wife, and the two are united into one." This is a great mystery, but it is an illustration of the way Christ and the church are one. (Ephesians 5:31–32)

From the beginning, God established the marriage covenant in order to illustrate our relationship with Him. Jesus is portrayed as the groom in the New Testament and the church as the bride of Christ. Why is it that we not only excuse but also at times even encourage Angela-type behavior with our Groom? The apostle James is quite clear in addressing this matter.

He is speaking only to professing Christians in these verses:

> Your motives are all wrong—you want only what will give you
> pleasure. You *adulterers!* Don't you realize that friendship with
> the world makes you an enemy of God? I say it again: If you want
> to be a friend of the world, you make yourself an enemy of God.
> Do you think the Scriptures have no meaning? They say that
> God is passionate that the spirit He has placed within us should
> be faithful to him. Come close to God, and God will come close
> to you. Wash your hands, you sinners; purify your hearts, for
> your loyalty is divided between God and the world. Let there be
> tears for what you have done. Let there be sorrow and deep grief.
> (James 4:3–5, 8–9)

These words are strong. In fact, in a day when unfaithfulness in relationships is quite common, they seem almost too drastic—even over-
stated. In my younger years, I had a bad habit of making *overstatements*.
I would make declarations of extreme consequence, largeness, or even
affection that were unrealistic. The terrible consequences were that my
family and friends stopped taking me seriously.

I think we've all been guilty of this on one level or another. Young
parents will often tell their child, "You do that again and you will be disciplined." It possibly works the first or second time, but eventually the child
challenges that statement again and discovers there's no follow through.
At that point, the child stops taking seriously his parent's words. This same
reaction occurs in schools, businesses, government, the press, and among
friends and family members. Too often we take lightly the warnings that
are meant to protect us.

Tragically, this same mentality also translates over to our heeding the
warnings of Scripture. We must remember, God says what He means and
He means what He says. It's important to remember that all Scripture

is inspired by God (see 2 Timothy 3:16). So when we read what James writes, the One who is speaking is God Himself.

If we really take to heart what I've written here, it will cause us to tremble in a healthy way. A Christian whose loyalty is divided between God and the world is an *adulterer*. That's a strong word. There are many sins a spouse can commit against his wife or her husband—gossip, lying, stealing, yelling, rudeness, and so forth. Each is detrimental to the relationship and shouldn't be treated lightly, but none would be as severe as adultery. This is why Justin was so shocked and upset with Angela. He was betrayed on the highest level and she saw nothing wrong with her unfaithfulness.

The apostle James continues by saying that in being a spiritual adulterer, we make ourselves an enemy of God. This is terribly serious, and we are the ones who cause this. God has no desire for us to be His enemy because He deeply loves us. But when we give our love and affection to the things and ways of the world, we sign up to be God's enemies.

Can we take these words lightly? Can we pretend this statement of James isn't in the New Testament and ignore it? James wasn't the only one who wrote about this either. We'll discover Paul, who among all the writers of the New Testament had the greatest revelation of God's grace, also wrote along this line, as did the apostle of love, John. Peter and Jude did so as well. But most importantly, Jesus says these same things to the churches of Asia after His resurrection.

In the coming chapters, we will unpack at length the meaning of how spiritual adultery makes us an enemy of God. We'll find out that this attitude and behavior are indeed the kryptonite we've been discussing.

TAKE ACTION

God is a jealous God. Most of us have known for a long time that Scripture teaches this, yet many Christians don't take time to think it through, or somehow believe that it only pertains to the Old Testament. Nothing could be further from the truth. If anything, Jesus's sacrifice shows us His love is the love of the most faithful bridegroom.

So you can see that we should want God to be jealous, not casual, in His love toward us, and we should ask Him for the grace to love Him with the same passion and devotion. This is the only way intimacy becomes possible.

Examine your heart today. How exclusive is your love for Jesus? Ask the Holy Spirit to show you any other love in your life that threatens to become adulterous against God. If He reveals anything to you, make the necessary change. Reflect on your exclusive relationship with God afresh today and recommit yourself to Him, just as if you were renewing your marriage vows to Him.

9

ADULTERY AGAINST GOD

The words of the apostle James ("You *adulterers*! Don't you realize that friendship with the world makes you an enemy of God?") are strong, so much so that you rarely hear them in gospel messages in churches, conferences, or individual discussions. Yet how can we overlook them? It's not as though his statement is an isolated occurrence in Scripture, as this theme appears frequently throughout the Bible.

If we examine James's words and heed their warning, it will clear up any confusion or fear that lingers about them. Here's his full statement again:

> You adulterers! Don't you realize that friendship with the
> world makes you an enemy of God? I say it again: If you want
> to be a friend of the world, you make yourself an enemy of
> God. (James 4:4)

First, God does not make Himself an enemy to us. Rather, we're the ones who make ourselves His enemy. Either scenario is nerve-wracking, to say the least; however, there's a difference.

We all have observed conflicts between individuals that originated as one-sided. In other words, one party declares the fight and the other party, even though engaged in the battle, would rather not be. For example, in 1941 the Japanese chose to bomb Pearl Harbor, and in doing so they made themselves an enemy of the United States. America would not have chosen this conflict nor did they desire it, but due to their provocation, Japan suffered the wrath of a more powerful nation.

This is exactly what James is communicating. God has no desire to be in opposition to people—His children at that, but He will not shy away from this conflict if we insist on aligning with the world. The Greek words for "enemy" in these occurrences are *echthra* and *echthros,* respectively. They are identical in meaning—the only difference is that the first is a noun and the second an adjective.

Did the English translators use too strong of a word? Is "enemy" more toned down in the original language? No, not really. One Greek dictionary uses these words as definitions: enemy, enmity, and hostility (CWSB). Another reads, "to live at enmity with someone" (BDAG), and yet another definition is: "the state of enmity with someone" (LOUW-NIDA). I'm showing definitions from three well-respected dictionaries to solidify the fact that there is no reason to choose some other word than "enemy" in this verse. It's critical to know the seriousness of what is being said.

There is yet another indication of the gravity here. The fact that James pens this warning and then writes, "I say it again," means what he's saying is highly important. His duplication of the statement is an established form of literary communication practiced among ancient Hebrews. Even though most manuscripts for the New Testament are taken from the Greek, these were Hebrew apostles writing these Scriptures.

In English when we want to emphasize the importance of a word or phrase, we have several methods. We can bold face, italicize, underscore, use all capitals, or add an exclamation point for emphasis. These are all ways of calling attention to a word or statement that is very important. However, the Hebrew writers would write a word or phrase twice for emphasis, and they were always careful with their words, not given to overstatement.

So not only is James's warning serious and strong, it is emphasized as necessary. Simply put, we can't overlook it.

Adulteresses

So what specifically is James saying when he uses the word "adulterers"? First, he is not speaking to all humanity here, but only believers. We know this because he states repeatedly throughout his book, "My dear brothers and sisters." Second, adultery *against* God by an unbeliever is impossible, because an unbeliever has no covenant relationship with God.

Look at it like this: I'm married to Lisa Bevere, therefore I could not commit marital adultery *against* Jane Smith, because I have no marital covenant relationship with her.

The only ones who can commit adultery *against* God are those who have received Jesus Christ as their Lord and Savior. All others are alienated from God—far from Him and not in a covenant relationship.

The Greek word for "adulterers" is *moichos*. This word is actually feminine in Greek, however, the English translation is masculine. A better rendition would have been "adulteresses." The KJV and NKJV versions attempted to alleviate this discrepancy by translating it "adulterers and adulteresses." It would seem the translators of the NLT and other popular versions were challenged by the feminine aspect. Perhaps they didn't want readers to think James was only speaking to women. But, in reading the entire context of his letter, it's quite clear James was addressing all believers. Bible commentaries agree that James is not targeting women only, so why it wasn't translated *adulteresses* is a mystery—not just to me, but also to Bible commentators.

What makes it more of a mystery is the feminine word *adulteresses* better aligns with the overall continuity of Scripture. God often relates to His people through marital imagery, Him being the husband and we being His wife.

The Old Testament prophets frequently did this. Isaiah writes, "For your Creator will be your husband; the Lord of Heaven's Armies is His name" (Isaiah 54:5). Consequently, when Israel's faithfulness to the Lord was nullified by her idolatry, she was accused of committing adultery. Ezekiel writes: "I will punish you for your . . . adultery" (Ezekiel 16:38). God speaks through Jeremiah, "'You have been unfaithful to Me, you people of Israel! You have been like a faithless wife who leaves her husband. I, the Lord, have spoken'" (Jeremiah 3:20).

The prophet Hosea's entire ministry portrays the unfaithfulness of a wife to her husband. He is instructed to marry a prostitute. In this real-life illustrated sermon, Hosea represents the Lord, and his wife, Gomer, represents God's people. This was done so Israel could see clearly how their idolatry was no different than a woman committing adultery against her husband, not with just one, but several lovers. Israel was an *adulteress*.

John the Baptist continues this imagery of marriage by saying, "'It is the bridegroom who marries the bride, and the bridegroom's friend is simply glad to stand with him and hear his vows'" (John 3:29). Again, Jesus is the Groom and God's people are viewed as the bride.

Jesus does the same when He calls God's people "an evil, adulterous generation" (see Matthew 12:39; 16:4). The word He uses for "adulterous" again is the feminine noun, not the masculine.

The apostle Paul continues this imagery by saying we are the bride and Jesus is the Groom (Ephesians 5:31–32). So, repeatedly in Scripture we see God's people, whether it's in the Old Testament or in the New, represented as the wife in our relationship with God. Therefore, James using the feminine noun for "adulteress" is consistent with this well-established biblical pattern.

Idolatry Is Adultery

In the Old Testament, the declaration of Judah or Israel committing adultery against God was always connected to idolatry. Simply put, the people were unfaithful to God. When we think of idolatry, we think of building statues, altars, or temples for gods. However, when Jesus declared the people to be adulterous it was not about them worshiping an engraved image of another god. Rather, they had asked Him to prove He was the Messiah by showing them a sign.

If we look at James's declaration of God's people being adulteresses, it also was not in regard to them building statues, altars, or temples. Interestingly, what James is referring to here is much the same activity Paul had to address with the church at Corinth—discriminating against brothers and sisters (James 2:1–13); slandering or speaking negatively of others (James 3:1–12); exhibiting envy, jealousy, and selfish ambition (James 3:13–18); and desiring and pursuing their own pleasures (James 4:1–3). These activities all point to adultery.

Is the continuity of Scripture broken at this point? Are God's people being accused of committing adultery for something different than idolatry? The simple answer is, "Not at all." It's all connected and related.

It's at this point the modern church seemingly ignores the warnings of Jesus, Paul, James, and other writers of the New Testament. Simply put, we're dumbing down idolatry to simply apply to statues, altars, and temples of worship to foreign gods. The truth is that idolatry is relevant to modern-day Western Christianity. In fact, our idolatry may be more widespread than it is in nations where temples, statues, and altars are built.

It is my intention to show that not only is idolatry prevalent in our culture today, but it is indeed the same kryptonite that hindered Judah and Israel's success—the same kryptonite that Paul was addressing with the church in Corinth, the same kryptonite addressed by James and other New Testament writers, as well. In present times, it is the same kryptonite that keeps individuals and church communities from success in manifesting God's greatness to our lost and dying world.

The World's Motivation

Before addressing this idolatry head on, let's continue to examine James's bold statement. He empathically states that "you want only what will give you pleasure" and then links this motivation to aligning with "the world." A line is drawn in the sand that is consistent throughout the New Testament. Simply put, the world is motivated by self-desire. John the apostle says it like this:

> For the world offers only a craving for physical pleasure, a craving for everything we see, and pride in our achievements and possessions. These are not from the Father, but are from this world. (1 John 2:16)

In this text, John's words are all-inclusive; in other words, he's defining *everything* that is in the world. There are many idols, but they all fall under one of the categories found in this verse. To commit adultery with the world is to be *driven by the intense desire* of what will bring pleasure to your five physical senses or what will feed your self-worth independent of God. In other words, *your pride.*

The Message paraphrase says that it is "wanting your own way, wanting everything for yourself, wanting to appear important." This is the driving force of the world. It comes down to this posture: "I know what is best for me, and I want it."

What is ironic is that God wants, desires, and is passionate about what is best for you. This truth every one of us must settle firmly in our hearts. This is crucial because the world is like an extremely seductive lover enticing us away from God. The world allures by getting you to think what it has to offer is much better for you than what God has for you. This is why James emphatically states:

> "So don't be misled, my brothers and sisters. Whatever is good
> and perfect is a gift coming down to us from God our Father."
> (James 1:16–17)

James starts by telling us not to be deceived, misled, or drawn away by the world's enticement. His message is simply this: *There is nothing good for you outside of God.* Settling this truth in your heart will keep you from being drawn away. It doesn't matter how good something seems, beneficial it appears, happy it makes you, humorous, fun, acceptable it is in our society, sensible it appears, popular, or rich it will make you. If it's contrary to the written Word of God, it is not good for you. It will ultimately take you to a place you don't want to find yourself, and that is the way of death. "There is a way which *seems right* to a man *and* appears straight before him, but at the end of it is the way of death" (Proverbs 14:12 AMPC).

Paths are different for each individual and there are many routes that lead to adultery with the world, but they all have one thing in common: They *seem right—good*, beneficial, profitable, acceptable, wise. But if they are contrary to the overall counsel of Scripture, all of them end up aligning with death.

I truly believe this is God's reason for this warning:

> So listen to me, My sons, and pay attention to My words. Don't
> let your hearts stray away toward *the world*. Don't wander down
> *the world's* wayward path. For *the world* has been the ruin of
> many; many men have been *the world's* victims. *The world's* house

is the road to the grave. *The world's* bedroom is the den of death"
(Proverbs 7:24–27, I substituted the words "the world" for "her"
and "she").

Solomon writes this to warn of sexual immorality, but there is a
deeper prophetic message: Beware of the luring methods of the world;
their forces are strong and inviting. Why would so many nations, along
with Israel and Judah, fall so easily into its deathbed? Could we be so
naïve to think those forces no longer exist? Beginning in the next chapter,
we'll discover how real and prevalent they are.

TAKE ACTION

No one enters marriage with a plan to commit adultery. While the vows
may be intimidating, brides and grooms do their best to put their whole
selves behind their covenant promises. Why is it, then, that so many mar-
riages fail, some even failing because of adultery? The answers are complex, but at the bottom of it all is a failure to remain on guard against the
forces that destroy connection.

Your relationship with God is your life—literally. There is no life outside of God. Yet the world seeks to seduce us into adultery against Him.
The best way to remain on guard is to pursue God wholly.

What can you do to ensure you are giving God your all?

How is your schedule? Do you protect time for God in it, time to read
the Word, pray, and fast? Do you look for opportunities to serve God in
your church, workplace, or community? Do you work at your job in such
a way that it is worship unto God? Determine one way you want to grow
in adultery-proofing your relationship with God. Define your plan, write
it, and then begin to do it.

10

WHAT'S BEHIND IDOLATRY?

We need to unwrap the mystery of idolatry. It won't be quick or easy, but unraveling it will be revealing and beneficial on many levels. The greatest benefit will be acquiring the knowledge needed to detect it in our lives. It will give us the upper hand in our awareness of spiritual kryptonite. Let's begin by looking at its roots.

Recall from the first chapter in this book that God has "planted eternity in the human heart" (Ecclesiastes 3:11). Every person on the planet is born with this innate quality. Paul affirms this by writing, "Even Gentiles *(unbelievers)*, who do not have God's written law, show that they know His law when they instinctively obey it, even without having heard it. They demonstrate that God's law is written in their hearts, for their own conscience and thoughts either accuse them or tell them they are doing right" (Romans 2:14–15).

Here's the truth: Everyone instinctively knows God's ways, because they're written on our conscience from birth. This became obvious to Lisa and me while raising our four boys. As infants, even before being taught "not to," they would have a look of guilt after striking their brother, throwing food, throwing a tantrum with their parents, or other similar behavior.

Not only is the knowledge of God in each person's heart, but it's also evident in everything created:

> They know the truth about God because He has made it *obvious* to them. . . . Through everything God made, they can *clearly see* His invisible qualities—His eternal power and divine nature. So they have *no excuse* for not knowing God. (Romans 1:19–20)

Ponder the emphasized words in these two verses: "obvious" and "clearly see," which leads to "no excuse." Here's the reality: There's no justification for a human being to be ignorant of God. He has made Himself known to anyone who is honest and desires truth.

Have you ever heard someone ask, "But what about the person who has never heard of God in the remote parts of Africa? How can they be saved? How could God condemn them to judgment?"

These questions, often statements of protest, are cop-outs for what they already know or what they aren't willing to learn. In their conscience they know God is real, but reject that truth. What they aren't willing to know is that His knowledge is available to all who seek truth. If completely honest, the questioners would have to admit they are denying Him. The psalmist further confirms creation's nonstop voice declaring God:

> The heavens proclaim the glory of God.
> The skies display His craftsmanship.
> Day after day they continue to speak;
> night after night they make Him known.
> They speak without a sound or word;
> their voice is never heard.
> Yet their message has gone throughout the earth,
> and their words to all the world. (Psalm 19:1–4)

The knowledge of God's vast greatness is declared continuously throughout the entire world each second of every minute, each minute of every hour, twenty-four hours a day, and 365 days a year. Wouldn't you say that covers the "ignorant" man in remote Africa? A person can put on a façade and live as though they're ignorant of God's existence, but the truth is not only implanted in their hearts at birth but continuously speaks to them day after day, night after night. Unless someone has reasoned away, convinced themselves otherwise, and ultimately seared their conscience to the point of becoming a fool, they cannot escape His reality.

The Critical Juncture

The critical juncture occurs when a human being either chooses to seek the living God or "satisfies" this desire by turning to a *god* or *gods*, thereby relieving his or her conscience. You may now be thinking, *I live in the West, gods are not a part of our culture. We don't have statues, icons, temples, or anything along these lines.* Please stay patient with me; I will indeed show that the West has various gods, no different than any other culture.

How do these *gods* originate? We must keep in mind mankind has created all *gods* or *idols*. A human being is compelled to satisfy this inborn awareness of God, along with the need to remain in good standing with Him. If an alternate version of deity is created, then whoever crafted it determines what's necessary to please the god, and that deity will provide or allow whatever its inventor desires—all the while satisfying the inborn need to worship. Now listen to what Paul goes on to say:

Yes, they knew God, but they wouldn't worship him as God or even give him thanks. And they began to think up foolish ideas of what God was like. As a result, their minds became dark and confused. Claiming to be wise, they instead became utter fools. And instead

of worshiping the glorious, ever-living God, they worshiped idols.
(Romans 1:21–23)

The building of the images (the idols) is not the focus here, but only the consequence of a deeper problem—*not worshipping Him as God*. At this point it is crucial to establish what true "worship" is. If we think of the church's worship team leading a "slow song," we will totally miss the message here. The truest definition of true *worship* is not music and singing, but rather *obedience*.

As an author of several books, I've learned when I'm introducing a fairly unfamiliar term in a book, I have to give its primary definition when I introduce it, either by directly defining it or using it in a way that perfectly illustrates the word's meaning. The same thing is true with any author, and God is no different.

If you look at the first occurrence in the Bible of the word "worship," it's Genesis 22:5. Abraham is speaking to his servants, informing them as to what he and Isaac are about to do on the mountain. Abraham states, "The boy and I will travel a little farther. We will *worship* there." What was he going a little farther to do? Was it to sing a slow song to God, or gather some musicians and singers to lead a worship service at church? Not at all. He was there to *obey* what God had told him to do three days earlier—to sacrifice his only son.

The NLT uses the word "worship" in Romans 1:21, while a few other translations use the words "glorify" or "honor." All of these words are related. We glorify and honor God or any other authority when we obey. We degrade or dishonor when we don't obey. We can give lip service, brag and praise, write songs about, and so forth, but if we don't do what God desires, we insult Him, which is the antonym or opposite of worship (or honor).

There was a day God said to His people, "'I hate all your show and pretense. . . . Away with your noisy hymns of praise! I will not listen to the music of your harps. Instead, I want to see a mighty flood of justice, an endless river of righteous living'" (Amos 5:21, 23–24). Righteous living is obedience to His authority, not what we determine is godly living.

Under the old covenant, God instructed Moses concerning acceptable offerings to Him. There were a variety of sacrifices His people could bring Him as a form of worship: a lamb (see Exodus 29:39–41), a bull (see Exodus 29:10–14), grain (see Exodus 29:41), and many others. Also, they could burn a holy incense called frankincense in the tabernacle and temple as a form of worship (see Leviticus 2:2). Yet one day God said:

> "I will bless those who have humble and contrite hearts, who tremble at My word. But those who choose their own ways . . . will not have their offerings accepted. When such people sacrifice a *bull*, it is no more acceptable than a human sacrifice. When they sacrifice a *lamb*, it's as though they had sacrificed a dog! When they bring an offering of *grain*, they might as well offer the blood of a pig. When they burn *frankincense*, it's as if they had blessed an idol." (Isaiah 66:2–3)

He begins by identifying those who come under His blessing, those who *tremble at His word*. This describes someone who ranks obedience as the supremely important issue. They will be the ones He gives His attention to.

Then He turns to those who choose their own way to worship (obey) Him. Not only were their acts of worship not accepted, but also were equivalent to a human sacrifice (cold-blooded murder), a dog sacrifice, pig's blood, and blessing an idol. These actions are abominable in His eyes. If someone actually offered these detestable things or committed murder, they would have been cut off from the community of Israel or punished by death. That's strong and decisive! So obviously their worship was not worship at all, even though it was in accordance with the instructions of worship that were given in the books of Exodus and Leviticus.

The Message paraphrase states it this way, "Your acts of worship are acts of sin."

Remember these are His covenant people, the ones who received His promises. Why did they hear such foreboding words? Because of worshiping their way and not obeying Him. The same is true for us: We can sing songs to God, attend worship services, or profess our allegiance to God, even in accordance with the prescribed ways of the New Testament. But if we don't have the foundation of obedience, our worship is really not worship at all. Aren't we told, "You must live as God's obedient children" (1 Peter 1:14)?

The other root problem Paul mentions is not giving God thanks, or ungratefulness. If we believe we're entitled to a certain lifestyle, deserving of certain material things, or expect some sort of status, we are self-focused and, consequently, unthankful. After all, we've worked hard, planned, set goals, dreamed up what we've accomplished or created, so we have a feeling of pride in our own labor.

Consequential Behavior

These root attitudes of turning our inward desire to obey, honor, and give thanks to something other than God Himself are what facilitate idolatry in a person, community, or nation. Paul then states:

> So God abandoned them to do whatever shameful things their
> hearts desired. As a result, they did vile and degrading things
> with each other's bodies. They *traded the truth about God for a
> lie.* So they worshiped and served the things God created instead
> of the Creator Himself, who is worthy of eternal praise! Amen.
> (Romans 1:24–25)

Remember the root of all of this is a lack of obedience and gratefulness to God. Now we are worshipping (obeying) our fallen nature's desires. We are submitting to what was created but is now flawed and cursed. Our moral compass has been compromised and *truth is exchanged for a lie*. Now, perceived wisdom is in reality foolishness. What is regarded as normal by the world is actually not normal. This continues until what is truly *good* is now labeled as *evil* and what is truly *evil* is identified as *good*. We then read:

> That is why God abandoned them to their shameful desires . . .
> (Romans 1:26)

After this statement, Paul spends the next few verses, representing 137 words in the NLT, listing twenty-two offenses against God. A sampling of these offenses includes murder, backstabbing, hatred, greed, disobedience to parents, and homosexuality. The revealing fact is that Paul uses fifty-nine of his 137 words (approximately forty-three percent) to address homosexuality, but gives the other twenty-one offenses just a couple of words each, offering no further commentary. Why is this? Is God isolating homosexuality and giving us a license to treat homosexuals as worse sinners than those who participate in the other sins? Absolutely not! Rather, He is making it clear that an affinity toward homosexuality is one of the best indicators of a society falling headlong into idolatry. Let's return to Paul's words:

> That is why God abandoned them to their shameful desires. Even
> the women turned against the natural way to have sex and instead
> indulged in sex with each other. And the men, instead of having
> normal sexual relations with women, burned with lust for each
> other. Men did shameful things with other men and as a result of
> this sin, they suffered within themselves the penalty they deserved.
> (Romans 1:26–27)

A society that ceases to acknowledge, give thanks, and obey God will trend toward acknowledging, then affirming (approving), and eventually applauding (encouraging) sexual perversion, especially homosexuality. Paul identifies this behavior as shameful and unnatural.

The truth is exchanged for a lie, which ultimately leads to confusion over gender.

In January 2017, *National Geographic* magazine dedicated its monthly publication to what it termed "The Gender Revolution." The editors assembled an array of individuals to represent the different sexual or gender orientations that mortal man has created. The magazine consulted with leading experts on human sexuality from universities and colleges. Some of the terms used to describe sexual and gender preferences were: agender, queer, androgynous, transgender, cisgender, genderqueer, intersex, straight, bi-gender, intersex nonbinary, transboy, or transgirl, and so on. This sounds sophisticated, but it falls under the category of foolishness and deception.

The people who come up with these terms are viewed as smart, educated, and experts of the day. What will be our society's outcome with this thinking leading our way? Studies have shown that the United States government has spent over two hundred billion dollars on issues dealing with gender identities and homosexuality.[1] Can you imagine how many opportunities could have been created with these resources? The funds could have been used to improve public school facilities, strengthen police forces, make renovations to airports and other public facilities, and most importantly, help homeless people, single mothers, and the disabled. Yet this enormous amount of money was spent all for the purpose of choosing a sexual preference contrary to how God created humankind. Right from the beginning Scripture declares, "God created human beings

---

1. Mat Staver: Homosexuality Costs The Government Tens Of Billions Of Dollars Brian Tashman | April 16, 2015 12:40 pm - http://www.rightwingwatch.org/post/mat-staver-homosexuality-costs-the -government-tens-of-billions-of-dollars/

.... Male and female He created them" (Genesis 1:27). He is the One who decides our gender; He knows what is best because He loves us.

Yet this is all done under the guise of being wise, when in reality it's a foolish waste of resources. Worst of all, it's encouraging the wrong behavior and keeping people in bondage to a lifestyle they weren't created for.

As a society we've bought the lie that it is a "human rights" issue, thereby permitting a very small percentage of individuals to link it to discrimination based on race or gender. These are rights we should contend for, but that is not the same as those who identify themselves differently from how they were created.

This is the absurd behavior Paul prophesies will happen when we stop truly worshipping (obeying) God and being thankful. So why don't leaders speak up and expose these misguided beliefs and efforts? We've become afraid of the truth and embraced lies and deception. We've drifted into idolatry, and it's taken a strong hold over us as a nation.

Society may call this progress, but it's actually a digression into foolishness. Paul's words, written so long ago, reveal how sexual and gender perversion are all rooted in idolatry. He then lists further consequences:

> Since they thought it foolish to acknowledge God, He abandoned them to their foolish thinking and let them do things that should never be done. Their lives became full of every kind of wickedness, sin, greed, hate, envy, murder, quarreling, deception, malicious behavior, and gossip. They are backstabbers, haters of God, insolent, proud, and boastful. They invent new ways of sinning, and they disobey their parents. They refuse to understand, break their promises, are heartless, and have no mercy. (Romans 1:28–31)

You don't have to look too hard, do a case study, or take a social studies class to discover this type of behavior in our society. It's widespread, rampant, and destroying lives, families, and nations. This perverse behavior and its acceptance are behind social breakdown, breaches of relation-ships, and wars of all sorts.

If this all isn't tragic enough, Paul concludes:

> They know God's justice requires that those who do these things deserve to die, yet they do them anyway. Worse yet, they encourage others to do them, too. (Romans 1:32)

Government, media, television and movie producers, social workers, leaders, influencers, and all of society are perfectly aware of this contrary behavior to our Creator, yet they ignore what their conscience speaks and what all creation proclaims. And to alleviate the voice of their conscience, they encourage others to do the same, hoping it will quiet down the truth in their hearts.

All of the behavior listed above is the result of the root problem of idolatry—not giving God the worship (honor and obedience) and grate-fulness He deserves. God is authentically acknowledged by our behav-ioral response to Him, not merely by our lip service. This applies to all humanity, but now let's turn our attention to how this plays out with a person who's already in relationship with Him.

TAKE ACTION

Worship is the choice to obey, honor, and give thanks to God. When we forsake any element of this true worship, we expose ourselves to the de-ception that leads to idolatry. This is true for us individually and culturally.

The first declared act of worship in Scripture was when Abraham obeyed God by going to sacrifice Isaac. What has God told you to do? This could be something the Holy Spirit has challenged you with as you read the Bible, or it could be something He has impressed upon you that is specific to you.

How does this chapter change the way you think about this assignment from God? Take a moment now to ask God what steps you can take toward fulfilling that assignment today, and be sure to thank Him for choosing you to do this, for speaking to you, and for being with you as you walk out your worship as obedience.

11

BELIEVERS' IDOLATRY

Idolatry among people of the world is bad enough, but finding it among those who have a covenant with the living God is dreadful.

James refers to this type of idolatry as adultery. It's labeled this because we have a covenant with God, and just like a husband or wife who is unfaithful to his or her spouse, when we give ourselves to idolatry, we are unfaithful to our Husband, the Lord Jesus Christ.

King Saul and the Amalekites

Let's begin in the Old Testament and move to the New. Israel had a covenant with God originating with their father, Abraham. God had given Israel's King Saul a directive through the prophet Samuel: "'Now listen to this message from the LORD!'" (1 Samuel 15:1). There was no mistaking God's will; it was direct and to the point. The king was told to completely destroy the Amalekites—every man, woman, child, and animal. It was God's revenge for how Amalek opposed Israel when they were fleeing Egypt and were at their most vulnerable. King Saul immediately rallied and mobilized the army to attack Amalek. However, we read:

Then Saul slaughtered the Amalekites from Havilah all the way
to Shur, east of Egypt. He captured Agag, the Amalekite king,
but completely destroyed everyone else. Saul and his men spared
Agag's life and kept the best of the sheep and goats, the cattle, the
fat calves, and the lambs—everything, in fact, that appealed to
them. They destroyed only what was worthless or of poor quality.
(1 Samuel 15:7–9)

It would appear to many in Israel that Saul did obey the Word of the
Lord, yet right after this we read, "Then the LORD said to Samuel, 'I am
sorry that I ever made Saul king, for he has not been loyal to Me and has
refused to obey My command'" (1 Samuel 15:10–11). Saul did not give
God the worship, the obedience He deserved. He wasn't faithful to God.

I recall a perplexed dad confiding in me that one of his greatest challenges with his teenage son was that the young man partially did what he
was told to do, but then he went off and did what he wanted, which usually was hanging out with his friends. When the father confronted him,
his son would get angry and retort, "Come on, Dad, quit being so hard on
me! I did ninety percent of what you told me to do. Why are you so picky?
Why don't you look at the ninety percent I did, instead of the ten percent
I *didn't* do?" The father was frustrated.

I said to the dad, "Then God is picky too." I reminded him of this incident with the Amalekites. I told him there must have been at least one
hundred thousand men, women, and children that Saul killed. I'm sure he
also slew many more sheep, goats, and cattle than he spared. So we could
safely say that Saul did more than ninety percent of what God told him to
do, yet God said that Saul had disobeyed him and later went on to use the
word "rebellion" in identifying Saul's behavior (verse 23).

This biblical background helped the father know he was truly sensing
incorrect behavior in his son.

In fact, I'm sure King Saul was closer to doing ninety-nine percent of what God told him. Why didn't God focus on all that Saul did, rather than the one percent he didn't do? This would be quite picky in most people's eyes, but to God, partial obedience—even almost complete obedience—is not obedience at all, but rather it is rebellion. It is not giving God the place of honor or worship due to Him.

Samuel then confronts Saul, who being deceived, flat out denies the accusation, but Samuel points out the animals that were being sacrificed. Saul then tried to put the blame on the people but Samuel corrected him, "No, you are the one in charge, you are the one who has disobeyed God" (paraphrased). Once Saul is backed into a corner by the prophetic confrontation, Samuel then states an amazing truth in regard to idolatry:

"For rebellion *is as* the sin of witchcraft,

And stubbornness *is as* iniquity and idolatry.

Because you have rejected the word of the LORD,

He also has rejected you from being king." (1 Samuel 15:23 NKJV)

For now, I'll focus on the second statement—"stubbornness *is as* . . . idolatry." Stubbornness means to "push" or "press." Saul pushed back from truth, from complete obedience.

The next words, "*is as*" in the verse are in italic type, which means they are not in the original text. There are no Hebrew words there, and the translators added them in to make it read better. The better translation would have been: "Stubbornness is . . . idolatry."

The reality is, when someone knows the truth, knows the will of God, knows what God has spoken, and yet pushes back and doesn't obey, it is idolatry. The reason? Their will, agenda, wishes, and desires have been placed above God's. All of these things come before Him, and an idol is anything we put before God.

Saul believed and even confessed, "I have obeyed God"; yet because he didn't fully obey but rather chose to put the people's desires (more accurately, his own desires) above the Word of the Lord, it was idolatry. It blinded him to his own contempt for the Lord.

Just as we saw in regard to all humanity in the book of Romans, of course the same is true for Saul. The root of Saul's idolatry was not statues, figurines, altars, or temples. Rather, it is not giving God due worship— obedience to what He reveals. This core behavior leads to unknowingly exchanging the truth for a lie, so deception began to take hold of Saul. It led him to "foolish thinking" and doing "things that should never be done." The tragic result of Saul's idolatry was that his life grew more and more in wickedness. He became jealous, demanding, unreasonable, full of rage, a hateful attacker of God's servants, a murderer, and even consulted a witch instead of God. These are some of Saul's consequential character traits, all resulting from the root of his idolatry.

Often those who have a relationship with God and yet choose their own desires over what He's clearly revealed through Scripture, become blind to their own disobedience. Just as it did with Saul, idolatry blinds us to the truth. We now have exchanged the truth for deception and believe God is on our side. We think He understands our heart and thus condones our behavior or approves of our lifestyle, when in reality we are in opposition to Him and have made ourselves an enemy of God.

Covetousness

I'll introduce the next aspect of idolatry by defining two key words. The first is "content" (contentment). It's defined by *Merriam-Webster* as "feeling or showing satisfaction with one's possessions, status, or situation." The Greek word most often used for content is *arkeo* and is defined as "to suffice, be sufficient, satisfy, and by implication to be strong and able to assist someone" (WSNTDICT).

We cannot properly serve unless we are content. Lacking this virtue will make us prone to view situations from the angle of *how will this benefit me?* Outward actions and words can appear unselfish or even self-denying, but if they are not founded in contentment, they will be fueled by self-serving motives.

Paul said to a church, "Not that I speak in regard to need, for I have learned in whatever state I am, to be content" (Philippians 4:11 NKJV). He did have needs, however; he'd just informed those he served that he was not seeking the gift for his benefit, but rather for theirs. He couldn't lie or exaggerate in writing the Scriptures, so we know this truly was his motive, not some "politically correct" statement. The only way his motives could have been this selfless is if he were perfectly content, even when he faced real needs.

For this reason we are told as believers, "Now godliness with *contentment* is great gain. And having food and clothing, with these we shall be *content*" (1 Timothy 6:6, 8 NKJV). There is "great gain" associated with contentment; however, the gain doesn't always appear on our timetable. Contentment helps us stay steady and not give up before we see answered prayer.

In prayer I asked the Lord for *His* definition of contentment. In my heart, I heard: *Complete satisfaction in My will.* Our Lord Jesus's life is the very picture of contentment. We hear this repeatedly in His words: "My food is to do the will of Him who sent Me, and to finish His work" (John 4:34 NKJV). His contentment with and commitment to God's will is clearly evident in the messianic Psalm, which reads, "I delight to do Your will, O my God, and Your law is within My heart" (Psalm 40:8 NKJV). No desire or passion existed for Him outside the will of God. His passion was to fulfill the desires of His Father.

Now contentment should not be confused with complacency, because they are nowhere close to each other in meaning. You will see Jesus "offered prayers and pleadings, with a loud cry and tears" (Hebrews 5:7). He threw over the moneychangers' tables, and He desired greatly to have dinner with the apostles the night before His suffering. He wasn't content to see people in bondage, sick, and lost; He was the Warrior on behalf of the oppressed. However, when it came to His needs or desires, He was content. He made His requests to His Father and believed His Father for provision.

From this contentment was born the words, "'I live because of the living Father.'" This produced an unworldly security and stability, so much so He boldly proclaimed, "'I know where I came from and where I am going'" (John 6:57 and 8:14). Because of this He could not be deterred or misled, and He was the perfect Servant!

Covetousness

The second key word related to defining idolatry is "covet" (covetousness); it is the perfect opposite of content. This is not a word you hear much in our everyday conversation, so it is important to identify it for the purpose of recognition and understanding in Scripture.

Let's start out with the English definition. One of Webster's is, "a strong desire of obtaining and possessing some supposed good." In turning to the Greek, it gets more descriptive. Before we do, let's first look at what Paul says leading up to mentioning *covetousness* in Colossians:

> If then you were raised with Christ, *seek* those things which are
> above, where Christ is, sitting at the right hand of God. *Set* your
> mind on things above, not on things on the earth. For you died,
> and your life is hidden with Christ in God. When Christ *who is*
> our life appears, then you also will appear with Him in glory.
> (Colossians 3:1–4 NKJV)

Paul is giving us the key to remaining in a *content* state. When we fully grasp we are in a covenant with Almighty God through Jesus Christ, we then realize we lack nothing—absolutely nothing. Jesus says that "the kingdom is ours," and if we seek first, not second or third, His kingdom, everything we have need of will be added to us.

This identifies the enemy's first major attack against Jesus. During the temptation in the wilderness, Satan attempted to get Jesus to seek provision outside of His Father. The conditions were daunting; after a forty-day fast, Jesus was very hungry. It was the enemy's hope to get Him out of being content to covetousness, but Jesus refused. Shortly afterward, the angels came and fed Jesus with food from heaven! The enemy's plan failed with Jesus, but that doesn't mean he won't use the same strategy against us. He targets us to move us from being content with the kingdom's provision to getting provision our own way.

Paul is saying that those who *seek* God, not just use God to get what they want from Him, but those who passionately desire His heart and pleasure are those who will find their minds becoming *set* on the things above. In this state we become like Jesus. Our passion is to do the will of Him who sends us. The fabulous result is that we now, like Jesus, cannot be deterred or misled and we are fit to be a genuine kingdom servant! Paul continues:

> Therefore put to death your members which are on the earth: fornication, uncleanness, passion, evil desire, and *covetousness, which is idolatry*. Because of these things the wrath of God is coming upon the sons of disobedience. (Colossians 3:5–6 NKJV)

Look at Paul's words, "covetousness, which is idolatry." Here is our next key in understanding what true idolatry is. It's easy to detect in pagan nations that have built the statues, altars, and temples, but it takes understanding and discernment in a "civilized culture." Paul says that when we move out of contentment into covetousness, we have moved from a relationship of intimacy with God into idolatry and adultery.

Let's now look at the Greek word *pleonexia*, which is translated "covetousness" in this verse. Let me give three different definitions from well-respected sources:

Pillar: "Inappropriate desire for more."

BDAG: "The state of desiring to have more than one's due."

CCE: "It implies a self-idolizing, grasping spirit."

Let's focus our attention on the final definition, "a self-idolizing, grasping spirit." When our affections are not set on the kingdom because we've not sought it first, we'll slip into self-survival mode. We'll now grasp for what we believe we need to be satisfied. We'll seek out pleasure, wealth and material gain, fame, status, position, reputation, companionship, ful-fillment, power, authority, lust, and many other wants from a self-idoliz-ing posture. We find ourselves in this state when we are not content. We strive because we lack peace and restfulness with what God has given us. We find ourselves in tension with His plan or process in our life.

Without a doubt, contentment and covetousness are opposing forces. Contentment moves us away from idolatry and closer to the heart of God, while covetousness distances us from God and drives us to the altars of idolatry. They are contrasting words with opposite meanings, which fur-ther illustrates their distinction. It's easy to see why the writer of Hebrews is so bold with the following statement:

> Let your conduct be without *covetousness*; be *content* with such
> things as you have. For He Himself has said, "I will never leave you
> nor forsake you." So we may boldly say: "The Lord is my helper; I
> will not fear. What can man do to me?" (Hebrews 13:5–6 NKJV)

We will discover in the next chapter that godly contentment gives us confidence in any situation of adversity. It keeps us from succumbing to the traps the world lays for believers. Contentment holds within itself great gain and a peace that transcends understanding.

In contrast, covetousness is a dwelling of unrest and is fueled by ceaseless desires and passions. It is a state where both deception and destruction are imminent.

TAKE ACTION

It's vital for us to clearly understand the truth of God's Word. It's written down for us, so we are all without excuse. None of us will be able to stand before God and be able to say, "But, Lord, I didn't know!" Just as He reveals Himself in creation to all peoples so they are without excuse, He has revealed His will in Scripture so that we are without excuse.

As difficult as it may be to hear that partial obedience is the same as idolatry, we can be thankful to learn this. If we know what's on the test, we can pass it every time. This is God's goodness and mercy!

Because it is so easy to become blind to where we have been partially obedient, stubborn, or covetous, ask the Holy Spirit to reveal any areas of your life that have come under this influence. Repent for any areas He shows you and ask Him to cleanse you. Finally, ask Him to fill your life afresh, empowering you to follow Him in obedience with your whole heart.

12

ALLEVIATING PRESSURE

In the previous chapter, I presented two different aspects of idolatry—stubbornness and covetousness. Now let's connect them, because they go hand in hand, and uncovering how they work together will bring us a step closer to understanding what makes a believer susceptible to kryptonite.

A Difficult Scenario

Consider again King Saul. He was not content to abide in the will of God. His stubbornness made him susceptible to covetousness. His first recorded error didn't occur with the Amalekites; it happened early in his reign when facing the Philistines. These enemies of Israel had gathered a massive army of three thousand chariots, which in those days were like tanks, and so many foot soldiers they appeared as numerous as the grains of sand on the seashore! They were camped at Micmash and were ready to attack.

Saul's military was nothing in comparison. It was newly formed and still getting on its feet. We read:

> The men of Israel saw what a tight spot they were in; and because
> they were hard pressed by the enemy, they tried to hide in caves,

thickets, rocks, holes, and cisterns. Some of them crossed the
Jordan River and escaped into the land of Gad and Gilead. Mean-
while, Saul stayed at Gilgal, and his men were trembling with fear.
(1 Samuel 13:6–7)

Can you imagine the pressure on Saul? You're the leader, commander,
and king, and your infant army is facing a much more experienced, powerful, and vast military. Saul's worst nightmare is unfolding right before
him—the men of his military are starting to go AWOL. However, possible relief is on the way—the senior prophet Samuel, who is scheduled to
come that day and offer the sacrifice to the Lord. This would renew the
men's confidence in Saul's leadership and give them courage to face the
battle. However, there's a problem:

Saul waited there seven days for Samuel, as Samuel had instructed
him earlier, but Samuel still didn't come. Saul realized that his
troops were rapidly slipping away. So he demanded, "Bring me the
burnt offering and the peace offerings!" And Saul sacrificed the
burnt offering himself. (1 Samuel 13:8–9)

It was no secret to anyone: Saul wasn't authorized by God to make an
offering. This action was reserved for the priest (Samuel was both prophet
and priest). But in fairness to Saul, in a pressure situation like this, he and
his men might have thought *desperate times call for desperate measures.*
Yet Samuel was about to straighten out any confusion over this matter:

Just as Saul was finishing with the burnt offering, Samuel arrived.
Saul went out to meet and welcome him, but Samuel said, "What
is this you have done?"
     Saul replied, "I saw my men scattering from me, and you
didn't arrive when you said you would, and the Philistines are at

Micmash ready for battle. So I said, 'The Philistines are ready to march against us at Gilgal, and I haven't even asked for the LORD's help!' So I felt compelled to offer the burnt offering myself before you came."

"How foolish!" Samuel exclaimed. "You have not kept the command the LORD your God gave you. Had you kept it, the LORD would have established your kingdom over Israel forever. But now your kingdom must end, for the LORD has sought out a man after his own heart." (1 Samuel 13:10–14)

This is what prophets do—clear out any confusion by bringing us back to what the Lord commands. People can easily forget what God desires during difficult times. Saul's actions of insecurity and discontentment communicated to the men of Israel that difficult times give us the right to choose whether it is best to obey God or not. This simply is not true! It is always most important to obey God, no matter what the times.

Saul's insecurity was simply a manifestation of his lack of contentment. He wanted everything around him to be under his control, and circumstances were far from that. He hated the pressure he was under and wanted it alleviated. His discontentment drove him to covet the peace he desired.

Here is the truth we all must come to grips with: In serving God we will often encounter adversity, hardship, and tribulations. Jesus guarantees it: "'In the world you will have tribulation'" (John 16:33 NKJV). Adversity locates the strength of our faith. If we find our faith flagging, if we are falling short on the faith meter, that's the time to cry out to God, to seek His Word, and to wait upon His Spirit. If we do these things, we will come out of the trial with a greater strength of faith than before.

Our faith is a precious commodity, more precious than any resources available on earth. Think of it like this: If someone offered you a failsafe business plan and the capital to invest in it, how would you respond?

Would you complain and say, "This is too hard or too much work!" Or would you jump right into the opportunity and hold a firm course on the failsafe plan? We absolutely would get started and expect a great return.

This is no different than what you face every time you encounter adversity that is bigger than you, and trust me, God will see to it that you get these opportunities. Not because He wants to frustrate you, but so that you can receive *the reward of greater faith.*

Another Difficult Scenario

Consider David, who was the opposite of Saul. He faced an even more daunting challenge.

He and his last six hundred friends on earth have all been rejected. It has not been a good day, but it is about to get much worse. They return to their homes in Ziklag only to find out that while gone, the Amalekites have invaded and taken all that was valuable—their wives, children, and resources—then burned all that was left. Nothing remained!

Can you imagine David's emotions? He's been in hiding in the wildernesses and deserts of Israel for over twelve years. He's not been able to see his family or childhood friends attend any worship services, enjoy community affairs, or any national events all this time. He's had to hide from and sometimes escape the finest special ops soldiers of Israel who've been tracking and hunting him.

Due to all this, it finally became so dangerous that he, his men, and their families had taken shelter in a foreign nation for two years. How long would this go on? Where was the reward of serving God? Several times David could have taken matters into his own hands and killed the leader in Israel God had put him under. This would have alleviated the pressure and his affliction. But he was faithful, persevered, and remained in a state of contentment for fourteen years.

Stop right there and think about it. Have you found yourself wanting to give up after three weeks of hardship? How about three months, or how about three years?

Three years is a long time to go through constant adversity; however, it pales in comparison to what David has endured. Saul's time period was roughly a week, and he gave in. He chose to pursue respect and greater status in the eyes of his men by disobeying God. He chose the behavior that would both alleviate as well as elevate himself. He didn't wait for the promotion that comes only from God.

Returning to David's story, he and his men return to Ziklag to find all that is dear and valuable to them gone. Upon discovering this, David and his men weep until their strength is gone. David may think he's hit rock bottom, but there's more. An even greater hardship is about to arise. Now his men, the last six hundred friends he has on the planet, are so angry they want to execute him!

> David was now in great danger because all his men were very bitter
> about losing their sons and daughters, and they began to talk of
> stoning him. (1 Samuel 30:6)

In his crisis situation, Saul's men went AWOL. He felt alone, in desperate need of affirmation, respect, and honor. He sought it out by compromising God's directive.

In contrast, David's men weren't deserting, but they wanted to kill him! David's situation was far more difficult than Saul's. Saul's discontentment led him to reduce pressure instead of trusting God by waiting for Samuel. David's response is quite different:

> But David found strength in the Lord his God. Then he said to
> Abiathar the priest, "Bring me the ephod!" So Abiathar brought
> it. Then David asked the Lord, "Should I chase after this band of
> raiders? Will I catch them?" And the Lord told him, "Yes, go after

them. You will surely recover everything that was taken from you!"
(1 Samuel 30:6–8)

David didn't try to talk his way out of this one, nor did he come up
with a presumptuous plan. He didn't say, "I've had it! What good is it
that I've served God faithfully? I've given Him my best years. He's the
One who put me under such a tyrant boss. He's the real reason I'm going
through a hellish life!"

David never blamed God. Nor did he covet the palace. In his hardship, David could have taken his revenge by killing Saul and promoting
himself to the throne God had promised to him. No, he waited on God
and Saul didn't. David remained in his pattern of contentment and chose
to ask God first.

God's deliverance or provision always comes, but not before the opportunity presents itself to disobey His Word—like the desert temptation
where Satan gave Jesus the chance to get out of His turmoil before the
angels came and ministered to Him. It almost always happens this way.
Staying in the place of contentment keeps us from seeking our own provision or promotion.

Back to the Amalekites

Continuing on with an examination of Saul's life, we turn our attention to
the incident with the Amalekites. On a timeline this, of course, happened
after Saul's encounter with the Philistines.

What fueled Saul's disobedience with the Amalekites? Why would he
spare the king's life and save the best animals when God's directive was
so clear? Once again, it's nothing more than covetous behavior, driven by
Saul's insecurity and discontentment in the will of God.

First, why spare the king? To conquer a nation is a huge achievement,
and in those days when kings were victorious in battle, they would often

bring the defeated king back to their palace. To have a king of a foreign nation you defeated in your midst was like having a living trophy. Every time you glanced upon him, it reminded you of your victory over his entire country. As often as your officials and palace servants beheld him, it reminded them of how powerful a leader you were. It was an ego and confidence booster, and this was beneficial, especially if you were an insecure leader.

Second, why not keep the best of the sheep and goats, the cattle, the fat calves, and the lambs? Again, it was for the same reason—Saul coveted respect and honor from his soldiers and people. If he gave them the best Amalekite animals, it would serve as a reminder of his great leadership. In times to come, they would reminisce and brag of his strength, strategy, and wisdom to attack the defeated nation. They would see that God was on his side and it would keep people from questioning his authority.

Saul's covetousness drove him to be continuously validated. He actually set up a monument to himself after this victory. When confronted by the prophet for his disobedience, he was more concerned by how his leadership team and citizens would view him, not that he'd disobeyed God (see 1 Samuel 15:30). In his eyes, the absence of Samuel—the most respected prophet in the nation—would dent his reputation, especially after Samuel had just corrected him. He needed to secure validation of his leadership and authority, which interestingly enough was given to him by God. He coveted respect, honor, greatness, and authority more than anything else. This covetousness led him to the stubbornness of his disobedience to God's directive.

Simply put, Saul was not content in the will of God.

A Source

It's now becoming clear that an idol becomes a source of something for us by fulfilling our covetous desires. This can happen in any area of our lives.

An idol takes the place God deserves. It can be the provider of happiness, comfort, peace, provision, authority, respect, and so forth. God says, "You shall not make idols for yourselves" (Leviticus 26:1 NKJV). We are the ones who make the idol, and it is not always made with stone, wood, or precious metal. The idol's power lies within our hearts.

An idol can be anything we put before God in our lives! It is what we love, like, trust, desire, or give our attention to more than the Lord. The Lord revealed to my wife, Lisa, that idolatry is what you draw your strength from or give your strength to. A believer is drawn into idolatry when he allows his heart to be stirred with discontentment and looks for satisfaction outside of obedience to God. This satisfaction could be a person, possession, or activity.

Hopefully, it is very clear now that idolatry is much more than figurines, statues, altars, and temples. Due to the fact that it's often been reduced to things like this, many miss some of Scripture's crucial warnings. In the coming chapters, we will continue to uncover idolatry's true identity and discover how prevalent and damaging it is in our twenty-first century Western culture.

TAKE ACTION

The basic element of idolatry is when you draw strength from or give strength to something or someone other than God. An idol becomes a source of something to us. This isn't going overboard to say that everyone should quit their jobs because they need to trust God to provide for them instead of their employer. But we need to recognize that God provides through our job.

We see that God provides love through our family, and we love them in return, but we recognize and honor God as the source. Most importantly, we honor God as the source of our life and as such, we reject choices that lead us away from Him.

Hopefully by now, you are beginning to understand how idolatry is more than just bowing to statues. Ask God to show you where idolatry has influence in your city or community, then intercede for those areas. Pray that God would shine the light of His truth into those places, send His children there as His light, and make Himself known as Lord of all.

13

KRYPTONITE!

Let's briefly revisit what we've covered in the past few chapters.

The heart of idolatry is not statues, figurines, altars, or temples. These are only byproducts of a deeper issue. Idolatry is humanity putting aside what God clearly wants in order to satisfy cravings or desires that are contrary to His wishes.

A warped view of God is the byproduct of this covetousness. Consequently, if anyone is engaged in idolatry, God withdraws and turns them over to their fallen nature to do shameful things from their corrupt natural desires. Enjoyment, pleasure, and pursuits gravitate toward what ultimately brings death rather than life.

This scenario is no different for the believer. A Christian engages in idolatry when he or she disregards what God has clearly revealed in order to obtain a strong desire. So, in essence, idolatry is *known disobedience* to the will of God. It's different than when a believer *falls into sin* and repents. Idolatry occurs when a believer is *given over to sin*. That man or woman has elevated their desire above God's will and formed an idol.

Idolatry is *spiritual kryptonite*.

If we look back and ponder the various examples discussed in earlier chapters, we'll conclude that the offenses were all along these lines. Achan was clearly instructed that everything taken from Jericho was to be dedicated to the Lord. Yet, when caught, he confessed, "'When I saw among the spoils . . . I *coveted* them and took them'" (Joshua 7:21 NKJV). The NLT reports his words, "I wanted them so much."

What Achan wanted was more important to him than what God required. He lacked godly fear and knowingly disobeyed. His intentional sin was nothing other than *idolatry*, or what we've identified as *spiritual kryptonite*. His idolatry not only brought judgment on himself and his family, but also crippled the community. Israel became weak and no longer could conquer other nations.

The Corinthian church frequently satisfied their own carnal desires to the neglect of what God had revealed to them. In fact, Paul writes that "you are still controlled by your sinful nature" (1 Corinthians 3:3). They were jealous, divided, quarreled among each other, committed and overlooked adultery, sued each other, and when they came together for the Lord's Supper, it really wasn't remembering Jesus. It was about satisfying their carnal appetites; in making this their focus, they knowingly disobeyed divine instructions. This is why Paul finally writes, "So, my dear brothers and sisters, when you gather for the Lord's Supper, wait for each other. If you are really hungry, eat at home so you won't bring judgment upon yourselves when you meet together" (1 Corinthians 11:33–34). Due to their covetousness (idolatry), many were weak, sick, and dying prematurely. They were not living as ambassadors of heaven.

The same thing is true of the people James wrote to. They were bitterly jealous of one another, motivated by selfish ambition, and quarreled and fought. James pointed out that they "covet and cannot obtain" (James 4:2 NKJV). Once again, we see believers practicing sin to satisfy their selfish desires. They were called "adulteresses" because they'd entered into idolatry. It wasn't because they built statues, figurines, temples, or altars. Even though it isn't mentioned, the spiritual kryptonite they tolerated most likely kept them from living supernaturally.

Idolatry is not merely sin; it's *intentional* or *known* sin. In essence, what we judge to be important, we will possess or do no matter what God has said about it.

This is how it all began in the garden. Adam and Eve coveted what they perceived was good, beneficial, profitable, pleasant, and would make them wise. They deliberately disobeyed what God had clearly spoken.

Once we've chosen this course of action, deception sets in. Now we fully believe we are still in good standing with God, when in reality we aren't. God will then have to send us a messenger—an apostle, prophet, pastor, or friend who loves us and cares enough to speak the truth. Even in doing so, at that point the deception has gained a stronghold, and though it can be broken, it is hard to break free. The first chapter of Romans states that those who engage in this type of behavior "suppress the truth by their wickedness" (verse 18). The truth about God and His ways are held back, so it's now harder to perceive and understand. Consequently, those involved "began to think up foolish ideas of what God was like. As a result, their minds became dark and confused. Claiming to be wise, they instead became utter fools" (Romans 1:21–22). Truth now is elusive, and alternate or perverted teachings of God are formed that endorse sin and misrepresent the way of life.

It's no different for a believer who enters into idolatry. Hear what James says: "But be doers of the word, and not hearers only, deceiving yourselves" (James 1:22 NKJV).

When we clearly hear the Word of God and don't obey it, something happens to us: a veil called "deception" covers our hearts. Now we fully believe we are right in our view of God, Jesus, and the kingdom, but in reality we are out of sync with God. The word "deceive" is defined as "to cause to accept as true or valid what is false or invalid" (*Merriam-Webster*). I don't know if that puts a healthy fear in you as it does me, but I hope it does. Intentional disobedience is not something to take lightly.

We kid ourselves if we say we can ignore these warnings in the New Testament because all is covered by God's grace, forgiveness, and love. Remember the same God who reveals His grace, forgiveness, and love in the New Testament is the One who reveals the dangers of practiced disobedience.

We can't just pick out the Scriptures we like and ignore or even throw out the ones we don't like. This mentality is itself deception. We must embrace the entire counsel of the Word of God. Sadly, we are currently experiencing an epidemic of ignored truth in the modern church. It's not because God is withholding truth; it's because of the consistent idolatry occurring in the church.

James goes on to say:

For if you listen to the Word and don't obey, it is like glancing at your face in a mirror. You see yourself, walk away, and forget what you look like. (James 1:23–24)

People who hear the Word of God and don't obey it will forget who they are in Christ. They will behave one way in church, a small group, or a conference, where the Word of God is spoken, yet walk out of these settings and act absolutely no differently than someone of the world. The Word of God is the mirror, so when they are in front of it they behave accordingly. Consequently, we have to come up with a skewed teaching to explain why it's okay to behave no differently than those of the world. We might say, "Well, Christians are really no different than unbelievers, we are just forgiven." Or we say, "God knows we have a fallen nature and we'll never in this life be able to walk in outward holiness. That's why He's covered us with His grace."

We can find supporting Scriptures in isolated places in the New Testament that appear to affirm these statements, but we have to throw out many others to actually believe this errant theology.

We have to decide:

- Do we really want to live in the mire of sin?
- Do we want kryptonite's effects to hinder our strength as super-natural ambassadors of God?
- Do we desire to abide far below what we've been created for in order to hang on to these deceptive teachings?
- Do we merely want to live no differently than the world and eventually just escape from this life and go to heaven?
- Or do we want to see the kingdom advanced, fulfilling the vision of the glorious latter temple (church) that we saw a few chapters ago?

In embracing kryptonite we give up our vigor, vitality, otherworldly powers, and ability to turn the world upside down. We in essence suppress the truth. We hold it back and hide Jesus from the rest of the world. This is why Paul finally cries out to the Corinthians:

Think straight. Awaken to the holiness of life. No more playing fast and loose with resurrection facts. Ignorance of God is a luxury you can't afford in times like these. Aren't you embarrassed that you've let this kind of thing go on as long as you have? (1 Corinthians 15:34 MSG)

He is telling this church that they have the ability to live like Jesus; however, they are still engaged in their idolatry. They still believe holding on to what's important to them is worth ignoring the revealed truth of the Word of God. They've played loose with the Word of God, suppressed the truth in their own lives, and as a result are crippled, have no power, and are not changing their society.

It's tragic on so many levels, but the worst part is that those who are lost and surround these idolaters have no manifested representation of Jesus. In the NKJV this verse is recorded: "Awake to righteousness, and do not sin; for some do not have the knowledge of God. I speak this to your shame." Paul is saying to this church, "You are the only Jesus the lost in Corinth will see. If they don't see the evidence of His resurrection power and nature in you, they just will not see it. Why have you suppressed the truth, not only to yourselves and the church, but also to the unsaved in your community?"

When we are synchronized with God, we are in harmony with life itself.

Have you wondered why the lost around us are not attracted to us, or if they are it's because the wrong thing appeals to them? Are they charmed only by our humor, our clever ways, our relevant fun, our entertainment, or our music? Or do they foremost see a living powerful King in and among us? Think of the early church; they were constantly identified as "gods" and were forced to fall down and essentially cry out, "No we aren't! We are the children of the Most High God."

Peter had to strongly say to an officer of the Roman military, "'Stand up; I myself am also a man'" (Acts 10:26 NKJV).

Paul had to cry out to all the citizens of Lystra, "'What do you think you're doing! We're not gods!'" (Acts 14:14–15 MSG).

In Malta, the citizens "jumped to the conclusion that he [Paul] was a god!" (Acts 28:6 MSG).

The "evening news" in Thessalonica reported, "'These who have turned the world upside down have come here too'" (Acts 17:6 NKJV).

It was stated by the citizens of Jerusalem, "All the people had high regard for them" (Acts 5:13).

These reports were lacking in Corinth, and they are lacking in our Western society. Is it because we've settled for kryptonite? I believe we've settled for the equivalent of a broken iPhone that cannot text. We'd rather be told the phone is permanently busted, so we can accept surviving without it.

I'm not one for settling. I'm not for losing our God-given vitality, life, strength, health, and ability to show the lost world a living Savior and King. I believe there are many who are fed up with merely existing—with barely surviving.

I sense a divine urgency, a commissioning from God to write this to you. It's for you if you are not satisfied with living in the filth, scum, and waste of this present world. It's for you if you desire a higher life, the resurrected life.

God your Father wants it for you—no, He's *passionate* about you living this higher life! He wants you to experience His divine nature and power more than you desire it.

God's not holding us back. If we're held back, it's because of our own idolatry.

III

As we move forward, we will look more deeply into the deception that has blinded so many in the modern church. We will see that what we have embraced as normal Christianity is not normal by heaven's standards.

We have a calling, a destiny, and an appointment with greatness that is waiting for us. It's time to shake off our disobedience and lethargy and be clothed with greatness, glory, majesty, and power—in Jesus Christ.

TAKE ACTION

Idolatry begins when we harden our hearts to what God says. This is the root of all idolatry. It is why God told Israel to rend their hearts and not their garments. He didn't want superficial repentance that failed to touch the root of the issue—their hard hearts that no longer heard or heeded His voice.

Deuteronomy 8 tells us this was the reason He disciplined Israel, that they would know that man does not live by bread alone, but by every word that comes from the mouth of God. Living from God's words, making His voice the source of our life, is what safeguards us from idolatry and propels us into the powerful life He calls us to live.

What role does God's voice have in your life? When was the last time you sought His input regarding your decisions? When you pray, is it one-sided, or is it a conversation? Take time right now to invite God to have a conversation with you. Be still and listen for His voice. Interact with Him, and when you are finished, write down what He says to you.

14

SIN

Sin. Do we dare tackle discussing it? Is it too controversial? Yet why wouldn't we want to be aware of our enemy so that we can take proper measures to master it?

Sin is a word many times used loosely or often avoided in conversations or messages due to the pain that may have been inflicted by legalistic accusations, teachings, or preaching. So let's look at it in the light of Scripture.

It's your sins that have cut you off from God. (Isaiah 59:2)

The Hebrew word for "sins" is *awon*. It is one of the four main words indicating sin in the Old Testament. However, according to the WSOT-DICT, this word "indicates sin that is particularly evil, since it strongly conveys the idea of twisting or perverting deliberately." It's *intentional* sin or as we've labeled it, *spiritual kryptonite*, and it separates us from God. It alienates us from divine virtues, which are required to live a godly life. When we engage in sin without sorrow, we've entered into idolatry and have become an adulteress. We've put ourselves in enmity against God.

The New Testament word for "sin" is *hamartia* (its companion verb is *hamartano*). These two words are used most frequently in the New

Testament to identify sin. The WSNTDICT states the one who engages in *hamartia* is "missing the true end and scope of our lives, which is God."

Stop reading for a moment and ponder this! When we sin, in essence we get off the course that (in our right mind) we'd never want to veer from. We deviate from the Source of all life—missing out on joy, peace, wisdom, satisfaction, contentment, provision, and more . . . the list is almost endless.

Many teachers define sin as *missing the mark*. This is accurate, however, when you consider the basic definition I've just presented, do you think "missing the mark" adequately describes the serious nature of sin?

There are other terms used for variations of sin in the New Testament, such as iniquity, transgression, injustice, and violation. However, it is not my intent to do a study on each, but to elaborate on the major aspects of sin and its power to lure people away from the source of true life.

Sin attacks our vitality, love, strength, soundness of mind, passion, and purpose. Make no mistake about it, sin is harmful and detrimental. It may indeed be pleasurable, but only for a season. In essence, engaging in sin is exchanging a short-term positive for a long-term negative, for after it's over sin stings us with the long-term consequences of death. Our flesh gravitates toward it, but as a new creation in Christ possessing God's nature, we internally have no desire for it and can resist its draw.

God told Cain, "Sin is crouching at the door, eager to control you. But you must subdue it and be its master" (Genesis 4:7). Notice there is a door for sin to enter into a person's life. That door is called "desire," and James writes, "These desires give birth to sinful actions" (James 1:15). This door is either shut or opened according to the decisions we make regarding desires. Sin is eager to control us. It too has desire, and its desire is to make us slaves. Jesus warns, "'Most assuredly, I say to you, whoever commits sin is a slave of sin'" (John 8:34 NKJV).

Paul elaborates Jesus's words to us believers: "Don't you realize that you become the slave of whatever you choose to obey? You can be a slave to sin, which leads to death, or you can choose to obey God, which leads to righteous living" (Romans 6:16). And if that's not enough, Peter also chimes in regarding practiced sin: "For you are a slave to whatever controls you" (2 Peter 2:19). Slavery is not a pretty thing and sin is a ruthless taskmaster. It's not to be dabbled with, but is regarded as deadly. It leads only to stronger desires and drives us toward what in the long run is harmful to us.

Sin is not obvious in its intention to enslave us. It's deceitful and controls us by hardening our hearts (see Hebrews 3:13), making it difficult to feel, sense, or hear the leading of the Spirit. Sin misleads us into harmful idolatry. Recall that God appeared to Solomon twice. Can you imagine that! Yet he worshipped false gods later in his life. You may think, *How could someone who has seen God turn to false gods*? The answer is through deceit. If it could happen to Solomon who saw God, how easily can it happen to those who have not seen God?

Sin is not something to mess with. It is very powerful and can change a heart quickly. The scary thing is that in a hardened state, our hearts are now deceived and we believe we are right when in reality we are not. We are now blind to our own depravity. Don't ever believe the lie, "I'm covered by grace; if I sin, I'll be fine in the long run." That attitude is playing with fire. Let me explain.

Intentional Sin Leads to Practiced Sin

Intentional sin eventually becomes *practiced* sin. Here's how this process occurs. When we first disobey, our conscience speaks to us. It's usually not a voice, rather an uncomfortable feeling. Our heart is screaming in a nonverbal language, "You have missed the mark, you have veered off the path of life, and you should make a course correction by repenting and asking forgiveness!" If at that point we forsake our sin through genuine repentance, our heart is cleansed and we remain sensitive to the voice of the Spirit. In Scripture we are told, "People who conceal their sins will not prosper, but if they confess and turn from them, they will receive mercy" (Proverbs 28:13).

However, if we ignore the voice of our conscience, the veil (discussed in the previous chapter) covers our heart. Now when we disobey again, we don't have such a deeply uncomfortable feeling. Rather, it's a smaller voice, an inward "pinch of discomfort," so to speak. It's harder to hear because our conscience has grown less sensitive. Yet we can still ask for forgiveness and be restored, if we've truly had a change of mind and heart toward the sin committed.

But if we still ignore this smaller voice of conviction in our conscience, then another veil comes over our heart, and our ability to perceive grows even weaker. When we disobey God's Word, there is now only a very faint inward tingle of discomfort. It's much harder to hear because our conscience is close to being completely desensitized. We can still ask for forgiveness and be restored if we've truly changed our mind and heart toward the sin, but it's very difficult to perceive our error.

If we once again ignore this faint voice of conviction, yet another veil covers our heart. As this process continues, our conscience eventually becomes seared or blinded to our idolatry. We move past feeling and become completely insensitive to the Spirit. We can now regularly sin without any feeling of conviction. We are in the state of *practicing* sin. We can still receive forgiveness and be restored; however, we will have little desire to do so, because we no longer see our sin as sin.

The next step is that God will send us a prophet, pastor, or friend to reach us. If we don't listen to the messenger, then the next step God uses to reach us is difficult circumstances, hardship, even affliction to get our attention. David states, "Before I was afflicted I went astray, but now I keep Your word" (Psalm 119:67 NKJV).

Let's face it; the best way for us to learn from God is to stay obedient to what He reveals to us, to stay away from sin. But if we don't, He loves us so much, He'll use hardships to teach us and get us back on the path of life. In the *New Living Translation*, David's words read, "I used to wander off until You disciplined me; but now I closely follow Your word."

If we review again Paul's words to the Corinthians, we will see the same description of the divine attempt to draw us back. He states to the Corinthian church, "Yet when we are judged by the Lord, we are being disciplined so that we will not be condemned along with the world" (1 Corinthians 11:32). It's God's hope that our hardship, affliction, or trouble He's allowed us to suffer will arrest our attention so that we will turn from the path of death back to the way of life.

We see this same concept when the apostle Paul speaks of the man who was sleeping with his stepmother. He states, "You are to deliver this man over to Satan for physical discipline [to destroy carnal lusts which prompted him to incest], that [his] spirit may [yet] be saved in the day of the Lord Jesus" (1 Corinthians 5:5 AMPC). This church father, in stating "you must throw this man out," was giving this directive not only to protect the Corinthian church from the corruption of this fast-spreading sin, but for the sake of the man who was in sin.

God loves His children deeply and dearly. This is why He will attempt to reach us in various ways depending upon where we are in regard to sin's slavery. In essence, He prioritizes the reality of what's best for our lives above our present comfort.

In the book of Hebrews, there's a statement that gives keen insight to the operation of sin:

Let us strip off every weight that slows us down, especially the sin that so easily trips us up. (Hebrews 12:1)

Notice his words, "that so easily trips us up." What may be a sin that easily trips me up may not be a sin that easily trips you up. For me it wasn't drunkenness, greed, drug addiction, gossip, or other obvious sins.

It was pornography. This was the greatest battle of my life, and I'll share in a later chapter how in 1985 I finally became free from this cruel slavemaster. The important point here is, we should know what temptations we are most susceptible to, and we must do what is necessary to cut off their opportunity. Jesus says it like this:

> If your hand causes you to sin, cut it off. It is better for you to enter into life maimed, rather than having two hands, to go to hell, into the fire that shall never be quenched. . . . And if your foot causes you to sin, cut it off. . . . And if your eye causes you to sin, pluck it out. (Mark 9:43, 45, 47 NKJV)

Jesus is not saying to literally cut off your hand or foot or pluck out your eye. What He is communicating is that we are to cut off the opportunity of the sins that easily trip us up.

I have numerous friends who were formerly alcoholics, and I had the privilege of helping one of them out of his addiction. He refuses to even take a sip of wine and is now very careful to stay out of any environment that promotes drinking. My friend knows this is an area of sin that can easily enslave him. He is wise in submitting to the words of Christ to cut off any opportunity to be enslaved.

On the other hand, before I was a Christian, during my university years, I drank and got drunk with my fraternity brothers and friends. However, one Christmas break I was at a bar and my friends drank themselves silly. When I arrived home at 12:30 a.m. after dropping off my drunken friends at their homes, I discovered my mom was waiting up for me. I told her about the evening and then blurted out in a matter-of-fact tone, "Mom, I don't even like drinking."

She laughed and said, "You are such a Bevere."

At that moment I realized I had never seen my dad drunk a day of his life. Drunkenness didn't run in his family, and that wasn't a sin that easily tripped Beveres up, although there were other sins that did. These are the sins which we must cut off any opportunity for them to gain entrance.

The writer of Hebrews then adds:

And have you forgotten the encouraging words God spoke to you as His children? He said, "My child, don't make light of the LORD's discipline, and don't give up when He corrects you. For the LORD disciplines those He loves, and He punishes each one He accepts as His child." (Hebrews 12:5–6)

The Lord disciplines us when we engage in sin. Let's briefly review His process: The first step is to correct us with His Word through conviction in our heart. If we don't listen—thus allowing veils to cover our conscience—then the conviction will come through a friend, pastor, or prophet. If we still don't listen, He will use hardship, adversity, or affliction.

Consider this: why would he write in the above verse, "don't give up" when God disciplines, which must be difficult? Listen to what's next:

But God's discipline is always good for us, so that we might share in His holiness. No discipline is enjoyable while it is happening—it's painful! But afterward there will be a peaceful harvest of right living for those who are trained in this way. (Hebrews 12:10–11)

Notice that the discipline is painful! There is no dumbing this down; God is not afraid to use the "rod of correction" with His children. So think of how stupid we are to choose to follow desires contrary to God. Think of it: We can enjoy a lot less pain by staying clear of sin, rather than enjoying its pleasure for a short season.

The Spirit of God was reaching out to the Corinthians through the apostle Paul, even to the man who was committing adultery with his father's wife. God continues to do so in the hopes of steering us back to the path of life so that we can be partakers of His holiness. There are no two ways around this. Either we can enjoy fullness of life by staying obedient to the Word of God or we can choose to veer toward idolatry—the intentional sin (spiritual kryptonite) that produces a lot of pain and suffering in the long run.

TAKE ACTION

By nature, sin is deceptive. It deceives about how fulfilling the sin will be. It deceives about how in control of the sin we are, rather than understanding how controlled by it we will become if we remain in it. But most of all, sin deceives because it distracts us from both the true glory we are called to live in and hinders us from experiencing a vibrant relationship with Christ.

But if we are filled with a vision of what God makes possible for our lives—the power, supernatural effectiveness, freedom, and intimacy with Him, and so much more—it helps us recognize sin for the counterfeit deception that it is.

Ask God to show you any area of your life where you have begun losing vision for the life He desires for you, areas where perhaps sin and compromise may be starting to look more appealing. Let Him show you fresh vision for those areas of your life and write down what He shows you.

EFFECTS OF KRYPTONITE

SECTION 3

15

THE STRENGTH OF SIN (PART 1)

In the Old Testament, Cain was warned, "Watch out! Sin is crouching at the door, eager to control you. But you must subdue it and be its master" (Genesis 4:7). The same scenario is true for any human being. Sin desires us; it wants to enslave and control us in order to express itself. Sin is a deceitful, seductive, and powerful foe.

So how do we master sin? The answer is through obedience to God's will, Word, and ways. Look again at what God says to Cain just prior to Genesis 4:7: "You will be accepted if you do what is right. But if you refuse to do what is right, then watch out! Sin is crouching at the door." Genuine obedience slams the *door of desire* to sin.

Recall Paul's words to believers (keep in mind, he's the man who received the deepest revelation of God's grace):

> Don't you realize that you become the slave of whatever you choose to obey? You can be a slave to sin, which leads to death, or you can choose to obey God, which leads to righteous living. (Romans 6:16)

Paul's words are similar to what was spoken to Cain. However, there is one huge difference. In the Old Testament, people's spirits were dead.

There was no life force flowing from their inner person. In the New Testament and now, the spirit in a person who believes in Jesus is alive; they are one with God and possess His divine nature. Therefore, we can choose to obey our inner person, our spirit, or we can choose to obey our outer person, our flesh.

The grace of God also comes into play; it not only saves and forgives us, but also strengthens us to obey truth. We are exhorted, "Let us have grace, by which we may serve God acceptably" (Hebrews 12:28 NKJV). Grace enables us to obey God.

Peter writes, "May God give you more and more *grace* . . . . By his divine power (*grace*), God has given us everything we need for living a godly life" (2 Peter 1:2–3). In both verses, and many others in the New Testament, grace is depicted as an empowering force. We have a new nature energized by His gift of grace. This wasn't available to Cain or anyone else in the Old Testament.

So why are many believers unsuccessful in mastering sin? It's important to remember we can possess power, but if we fail to use it we won't benefit from it. God gives each of us the ability to choose, and He'll not override our choices. So when any Christian disobeys God, sin gains the upper hand on believers. Why would anyone allow this? This can only occur if sin convinces a believer that something desired is more beneficial than obedience to God, and it's for this reason Paul writes:

The strength of sin is the law. (1 Corinthians 15:56 NKJV)

This is a loaded and, perhaps, surprising statement: The *law* provides sin its power over a person. At first glance you may be thinking, *I'm not under the Law of Moses*! True, however, it's important to note that not every time the word "law" is mentioned in Scripture does it apply to the Law of Moses. James talks about the "royal law" (see James 2:8), which speaks of loving our neighbor. There is the "law of God" (see Romans 8:7

and Hebrews 8:10) that is written on believers' hearts. There is the "law of Christ" (see Galatians 6:2), which is fulfilled by bearing one another's burdens. And there is the "law of liberty" (see James 2:12 NKJV), which we will be judged by. And there are even more of these "laws." Paul is not discussing any of these laws or the Law of Moses in the 1 Corinthians 15:56 verse.

So what *law* is Paul referring to that gives sin its power over a believer? Allow me to illustrate before I identify it. Here are some typical thoughts or statements spoken by someone under the law Paul mentions: "I shouldn't watch this movie, because it contains nudity and swearing." Or "I need to tithe." Or "I shouldn't look at that woman across the room who's wearing the skanky clothing."

What kind of *law* do these statements identify? A person saying these things or the like is someone who is restricted by the Word of God, rather than it being his or her delight. He or she sees God's Word as constraining or binding, which is the antithesis of the psalmist's words: "I take joy in doing Your will, my God, for Your instructions are written on my heart" (Psalm 40:8). The person "under the law" doesn't passionately *will to do His will* (see John 7:17 NKJV).

In essence, this statement sums it all up: "I'd like to . . . but God's Word states otherwise." And there is a perfect example of this attitude in the Old Testament.

A Prophet Not in Sync

Balaam was a prophet. He knew God's voice, and the Lord's ways were not foreign to him. The king of Moab, who also ruled the people of Midian, was a man named Balak. The citizens of this king's entire realm were terrified because the people of Israel were moving toward them. The Israelites had just plundered Egypt—the most powerful nation in the world—and crossed the Red Sea. Egypt's military, agriculture, and economy had been devastated, along with every family's first-born son miraculously now dead.

After Israel had come out of Egypt, they'd encountered resistance from the Amorites and soundly defeated them, too. Now Israel was camped on the plains of Moab and the people, the leaders, and the king were all petrified, thinking that Israel would do to them what they had done to Egypt and the Amorites.

King Balak was informed of a notable and powerful prophet named Balaam, and that if he blessed someone, good things would happen. But if Balaam cursed a person, they were cursed without fail. King Balak sent his leaders to the prophet Balaam with an offering saying, "'Please come at once, curse this people [the Israelites] for me, for they *are* too mighty for me. Perhaps I shall be able to defeat them and drive them out of the land'" (Numbers 22:6 NKJV).

Balaam made this reply to the messengers:

> "Lodge here tonight, and I will bring back word to you, as the
> LORD speaks to me." So the princes of Moab stayed with Balaam.
> (Numbers 22:8 NKJV)

Notice Balaam's reference to "the Lord." He was not consulting some foreign god's direction, because he was a prophet of the one true God. The name he used for "Lord" is *Yahweh*. This is God's name, and the writers of the Old Testament never used this name to identify a false god.

How often do we refer to both Jesus and God our Father as our *Lord?* We are not speaking of anyone other than our Creator, Supreme Master, and the One who gave His life for us. Balaam also did just this.

Let's observe carefully what God said to Balaam that night. It's interesting to note He didn't even wait for Balaam to seek Him:

> God came to Balaam and said, "Who are these men with you?"
> (Numbers 22:9 NKJV)

The Lord was in essence saying to Balaam, "Who are these men to Me? They have no covenant with Me! Are you seriously going to ask Me if you should go and curse My covenant people? Why do you need to pray about this? Isn't it obvious?"

There are some things we don't need to pray about! We already know what the will of God is from what He's revealed in His written covenant. You don't need to pray about whether or not you should gather with other Christians. God has already said, "Let us not neglect our meeting together, as some people do" (Hebrews 10:25).

You don't need to pray about giving an offering to those who minister to you, for Scripture states, "The Lord ordered that those who preach the Good News should be supported by those who benefit from it" (1 Corinthians 9:14).

You don't have to ask if you can enter into, or to encourage another, in a homosexual relationship. God has already made this clear:

Don't you realize that those who do wrong will not inherit the Kingdom of God? Don't fool yourselves. Those who indulge in sexual sin, or who worship idols, or commit adultery, or are male prostitutes, or practice homosexuality, or are thieves, or greedy people, or drunkards, or are abusive, or cheat people—none of these will inherit the Kingdom of God. (1 Corinthians 6:9–10)

You wouldn't need to ask God if you could cheat on your taxes; that's stealing. Or move in with and sleep with your boyfriend or girlfriend before marriage; that's sexual sin. Or enter into a relationship with another man's wife; that's adultery—and the list continues on and on. We have many commandments in the New Testament that already make God's will perfectly clear.

In essence, God went on to say, "Okay, Balaam, since you didn't get the clue, or more accurately, didn't *want* to get the clue, I will make My will perfectly clear to you . . ." "You shall not go with them; you shall not curse the people, for they *are* blessed" (Numbers 22:12 NKJV).

No interpretation needed here.

Now observe Balaam's response to the divine directive:

So Balaam rose in the morning and said to the princes of Balak, "Go back to your land, for the LORD has *refused* to give me permission to go with you." (Numbers 22:13 NKJV)

Most would cheer Balaam. We'd applaud his obedience and say, "He's a godly brother!" However, there is a clue in his statement that would cause us to think otherwise. Notice he says, "The Lord has *refused* to give me permission." He doesn't say, "The Lord has made His desire clear; therefore I will not go." He uses the word *refused*.

Consider this example: A group of high school friends decide to go shopping and see a movie. Amy has asked her parents for permission to go. Their response is, "Amy, we are going to have a family night together, so we'd like you to stay with us."

Amy's friends drive up and come to the door to pick her up. When she answers the door, they say, "Ready to go?"

Amy's reply, said with a frown, is, "I can't go." In other words, *I want to go with you guys, but I have to stay home for family night.* She is being restrained by her parents' wishes from what she really wants to do. Her parents' words are *law* to her. This is exactly what Balaam said.

A Sweeter Deal

So the elders of Moab returned to the king and reported Balaam's answer. However, the king was not satisfied and would not take no for an answer. So he countered by sending more elders with greater honor and a larger offer to engage Balaam's labor. The king's exact words were, "'I will certainly honor you greatly, and I will do whatever you say to me. Therefore please come, curse this people for me'" (Numbers 22:16–17 NKJV).

If your next-door neighbor says to you, "I'll give you anything I have," that may not be a lot, but if a king of an entire nation makes this offer, wow, that's huge.

When I was in high school, there was a renowned comedian named Flip Wilson. One of his famous lines was, "The devil made me do it."

It was funny and people repeated it often, but his words aren't true. The devil cannot make a believer do anything. We are clearly told, "But each one is tempted when he is drawn away by his own desires and *enticed*" (James 1:14 NKJV). The key word is *enticed*. That's all the devil can do to a believer. But you cannot be enticed by something you don't desire. If you were to put a line of cocaine in front of me I would say, "Get that away from me." You couldn't entice me with it, because I have no desire for illegal drugs.

But the devil is clever and isn't slothful. He's not only assigned demons to study your life, they have studied your father and mother, and their fathers and mothers. He knows the weak tendencies in your family line when it comes to desire.

He had studied Balaam's life and knew this prophet possessed an unhealthy desire for riches, rewards, and status. I believe this is why Satan prompted this ungodly king Balak to make a more lucrative offer. But hold on, Balaam's response to the more significant offer was strong:

> "Though Balak were to give me his house full of silver and gold, I
> *could not* go beyond the word of the LORD my God, to do less or
> more." (Numbers 22:18 NKJV)

We again would applaud Balaam's bold stance to not disobey the Word of God, even when a more substantial offer is made. However, again we see key words that indicate the prophet's confinement. He said, "I could not" rather than "I will not." Nothing's changed. He was still being re-strained by the Word of God, which is law to him. His next statement affirmed this:

> "Now therefore, please, you also stay here tonight, that I may
> know what more the LORD will say to me." (Numbers 22:19
> NKJV)

What? Is a more lucrative offer going to change God's mind? Could anyone possibly believe God instructed him to say "no" the first time be-cause He knew the king would offer Balaam substantially more with the next ambassadors? What ludicrous thinking! God wasn't suggesting Ba-laam hold out for a better deal! So if Balaam didn't need to pray about it the first time, how much more this second time! And God had made His will clear with the first ambassadors, "You shall not go with them."

Even so, Balaam still chose to pray that night. However, hear God's response:

> "Since these men have come for you, get up and go with them. But
> do only what I tell you to do." (Numbers 22:20)

Wait a minute! God now says "go with them." Did we read this cor-rectly? What's going on? Surprisingly, the tables have turned! Balaam now has the word of the Lord to go with these princes and elders of Moab. So he does exactly what God told him to do. He saddles his donkey, and goes with the princes of Moab. He's obedient to the divine directive. However, look at what happens next:

> Then God's anger was aroused because he went. (Numbers
> 22:22 NKJV)

What's going on? Is God schizophrenic? Balaam is doing exactly what God instructed the night before, yet now God is angry at him for doing it. How can this be explained?

There is a logical answer found in Scripture and it's quite revealing. It revolves around the truth that *sin gets its strength from the law*. We'll discover why in the next chapter.

TAKE ACTION

Many believers need to hear this message of hope: You can be completely free from the power of sin.

Yes, you read that correctly. It's possible for Christians to rise above sin. Jesus did not die just to grant you a ticket to heaven. When He died, He set you free from the power of sin and death. Sin doesn't have power over you, but instead you have power over it.

This is only possible through God's grace—His divine power to accomplish something that is impossible in our human strength. We have free access to grace and possess this power, but we lose its benefits if we fail to exercise it. One of the most common ways believers fail to use this power is to not realize they have it.

Strengthen yourself against sin today by pondering the Scriptures that reveal you truly do have power over it. Meditate on this truth until it becomes a reality. Connect with God about this, repenting for any way you have given sin power over you and thanking Him for setting you free from that today. Forgive yourself for your past failures and ask God to show you how He sees your future. Write down what He shows or tells you.

16

THE STRENGTH OF SIN (PART 2)

Let's pick up where we left off with the prophet Balaam in the previous chapter.

After receiving God's instructions to not go with the first set of ambassadors from Moab and Midian, Balaam once more goes to the Lord with the second, more prominent, group of representatives. He's hoping for a different response.

Has this ever been your situation? Have you ever known in your heart what God was saying, but you went to Him in prayer anyway, hoping for a change in His response? You perhaps covered up the inappropriate desire by saying, "Let me pray about it," or "Let me pray about it one more time."

I don't know about you, but I've been guilty of this, and I'll share later in this chapter a couple of my sad experiences in this area.

Balaam coveted both the offering and the honor from this powerful king but didn't dare go outside of the "limitations" of God's instruction. He was smart enough to know that he couldn't be blessed if he deliberately disobeyed. Sometimes this is just enough knowledge to open the door to greater deception.

So you can imagine Balaam's surprise when God says, "Get up and go with them." Balaam may have thought, *Shocking! It's a good thing I prayed about this again!*

So Balaam got up the next morning and did exactly what God had told him to do the night before, and to our amazement we read, "Then God's anger was aroused because he went" (Numbers 22:22 NKJV).

What, is God schizophrenic? Of course that's a rhetorical question, because we all know the answer is, *no way!* Why then was God angry? Balaam had done exactly what God told him to do—he went. Then God became angry with him for simply going. So what's going on?

There is a truth revealed here that many do not know and understand, and it took me years of hardships before I discovered it:

> *If we really desire (covet) something, and God has communicated His will on the matter (whether through His Word or in prayer) yet we still desire it, God will often give it to us, even if He knows it is not best for us and that we will ultimately be judged for it.*

This statement may shock you, but it is true. Let me prove it with some biblical examples.

Fulfilled Requests

Israel wanted a king. The leaders approached the prophet Samuel and made their desire known. They said, "'Give us a king to judge us like all the other nations have'" (1 Samuel 8:5).

Samuel inquired of the Lord about their request, and God gave an answer for the leaders through the prophet, a warning of why having a king would not be good for them. He forewarned them that the king would draft their sons to his army. The king also would take their sons to plow his fields, harvest his crops, and make weapons and equipment for him.

He would also take their daughters and force them into the labor of cooking, cleaning, making perfume, and other various jobs. Not stopping with all that, the king would claim their best fields, vineyards, olive groves, cattle, and sheep, and give all of it to his officials. God then said the people would eventually beg for relief from the king they had desired, but He would not help them.

Next we read, "But the people refused to listen to Samuel's warning. 'Even so, we still want a king,' they said. 'We want to be like the nations around us'" (1 Samuel 8:19–20).

So Samuel repeated to the Lord what the people so passionately desired. God's reply to Samuel was contrary to His will. He says, "'Do as they say, and give them a king'" (1 Samuel 8:22). God gave them what they coveted, even when it wasn't best. They got their monarch, and he and the kings who followed did everything the people were warned of.

Here's another example. Israel came out of Egypt and God fed them with otherworldly food. It was called manna—bread from heaven, a food elsewhere in Scripture referred to as the "food of angels" (see Psalm 78:25). It was so nutritious that Elijah later ate only two cakes of it and ran forty days nonstop on its strength. There are times I would love to have food like this!

However, Israel grew tired of this bread and wanted meat. So they made a request. The psalmist writes, "They asked for meat, and he sent them quail" (105:40). God answered their request in a most amazing way. We read:

He released the east wind in the heavens and guided the south
wind *by His mighty power*. He rained down meat as thick as
dust—birds as plentiful as the sand on the seashore! He caused
the birds to fall within their camp and all around their tents."
(Psalm 78:26–28)

God not only answered the request, but He did it miraculously! By His *mighty power* He brought hundreds of thousands of birds into the camp. The Israelites didn't have to hunt them and didn't need dogs, weapons, cages, or any other devices to catch them. The quail just fluttered into the camp, and the people simply picked them out of the air or off the ground. If this happened today, the story would blow up on social media and dominate the news headlines. God came through big time, yet look at what the psalmist writes next:

> So they ate and were well filled, for He gave them their *own desire*.
> They were not deprived of their craving; but while their food was
> still in their mouths, the wrath of God came against them, and slew
> the stoutest of them, and struck down the choice men of Israel.
> (Psalm 78: 29–31 NKJV)

God, not a false god or demon, gave them what they *desired*, and did it miraculously, but before they were done eating, His judgment fell on them!

We must keep in mind that God decided before He created mankind to give us freedom to choose, even though He knew we could potentially choose what would ultimately be against His desire and even detrimental to us.

For example, how about the prodigal son? He asked for his inheritance, and his father knew he didn't have the maturity to handle it correctly. Yet, because his son desired it so intensely, his father capitulated and handed over the inheritance. The result was that the son ended up in deep sorrow in a pigpen.

There are other examples to give from Scripture, but I think you see the truth. *We are in an unfavorable and detrimental position when we passionately ask for something that is not the will of God.*

A Smart Donkey

With this knowledge, let's return to the story of Balaam.

He was now on the way to meet the king of Moab. The king's aides were accompanying him but God was angry at his choice. Suddenly, an angel took a stand against Balaam. Please keep in mind that angels are not little fat babies with bows and arrows but instead massive beings with great strength. I'm speculating that this one was in the range of eight to ten feet tall.

The Angel stood on the road ahead of Balaam with His drawn sword, and God miraculously opened the eyes of the *donkey*. Once it saw this massive being with a weapon ready to strike, she jumped off the road out into the field to avoid Him. Balaam, out of anger, struck his donkey and guided it back to the road.

The Angel then moved to a place on the road where there was a wall on both sides. The donkey once again, seeing the Angel, tried to go as far from Him as possible and crushed Balaam's foot between her body and the wall. Balaam became even angrier at the donkey and beat it again.

The Angel next went to a place on the road where the gap was so narrow that there was nowhere to turn. This time, when the donkey saw the Angel with his sword drawn, it lay down under Balaam. Now Balaam was really furious and struck again.

God then opened the mouth of the donkey, and it said to Balaam, "'What have I done to you, that you have struck me these three times?'" (Numbers 22:28 NKJV).

Balaam and the donkey had a heated exchange of words, and finally God opened the eyes of Balaam to see the Angel. He immediately bowed prostrate on his face.

Up to this point, I've referred to this angel as simply one of the myriad angels who serve before God. However, it is obvious the translators of the

NKJV, as well as myself, believe this angel was actually the Lord Himself. But I'll leave that for you to decide, as it is not my intention to convince you either way.

The Angel confronted Balaam by saying, "'Behold, I have come out to stand against you, because your way is perverse before Me. The donkey saw Me and turned aside from Me these three times. If she had not turned aside from Me, surely I would also have killed you by now, and let her live'" (Numbers 22:32–33 NKJV).

This donkey saved Balaam's life! He would have been a dead man if she didn't avert the Lord. You would think Balaam would say to the leaders of Moab and Midian, "Guys, I'm out of here. Tell your king he can keep his money." But that wasn't what he said. Instead, Balaam confessed to the Lord:

"I have sinned, for I did not know You stood in the way against me. Now therefore, if it displeases You, I will turn back." (Numbers 22:34 NKJV)

Balaam admitted his sin, yet he spoke out of the other side of his mouth by saying "if it displeases You."

Really, Balaam? What's it going to take? Even though the Lord Himself had come out to stand against him in a dramatic way, Balaam still tried to get what he wanted. He so coveted the money and honor offered by the king that he was oblivious to divine discipline. His idolatry had blinded him completely to God's heart.

This is exactly what happens when our desire outweighs obeying God, when we feel constrained by what He commands. The sin grows in strength through the deception. Now what is obviously out of sync with God is no longer apparent. The obedient see it clearly, but due to the grip of idolatry, even they continue to attempt to get God's approval for what is intensely desired.

My Shortcomings

When I was in my early thirties, God clearly showed both Lisa and me that entering an agreement with a certain well-known publishing company was not His will. I said "no" after the acquisitions editor approached me the first time, but not in a way similar to Balaam's first encounter with Balak's leaders.

The editor continued to call me almost on a daily basis. He said my message was important for the body of Christ and shared with me how other relatively unknown authors had published with his company and were now famous. I swallowed his flattery hook, line, and sinker. At the time, my two existing books were self-published and reached very few readers. I wanted the national reach and influence of this publisher. Even though God also wanted the messages to advance, it was not His time, the particular message, or the publisher. Besides this, my motives were wrong; I wanted to be known, which is identified as *the pride of life*—seeking status or reputation.

My desire to be published by this renowned company became so intense that I ignored the Lord's clear direction, my wife's counsel, and the signs of many things going wrong. The inward guidance of the Holy Spirit's warnings all faded and were replaced by the deception of greater desire.

The publisher was in a different state. We made the decision for Lisa to fly out and sign the contract on behalf of our organization because my schedule didn't permit it. The morning of her departure, one of our sons threw up all the way down the carpeted stairway to the second floor of our house. As we were cleaning it up, she exasperatedly said, "John, can't you see God doesn't want us to do this?!"

I boldly countered, "No, this is the enemy trying to discourage and stop us." If this was all that went wrong, I could possibly have been correct. But so much was going awry it was uncanny, and I could not see through it. I was deceived by the strength of my sin.

Lisa flew out and signed the contract that day. For the next three months, chaos invaded my life. Peace left me and struggling and striving took over. I was sick with different viruses, colds, and other physical ailments for three solid months. We had an awful time with the publisher, we couldn't agree on anything, and our ministry lost thousands of dollars.

I differed from Balaam in one respect; I finally saw how my intense desire had blinded my eyes to the will of God. I had been under the judgment (*discipline*) of God. Recall Paul's words, "That is why many of you are weak and sick and some have even died. But if we would examine ourselves, we would not be judged by God in this way. Yet when we are judged by the Lord, we are being disciplined" (1 Corinthians 11:30–32). It took a lot of unnecessary hardship to finally see the idol I'd created. I repented of my stubbornness and everything turned around, almost immediately. The publisher shortly afterward informed us they wanted our working relationship terminated.

Approximately a year later, another well-known company offered to publish a different one of my messages on freedom from offense. God spoke to me and said, "The previous publisher was your idea; this publisher is Mine." My motives had also changed from the chastisement I'd gone through a year earlier. I was now passionate to obey God, so people could be genuinely free. This was the message God desired and now that book, *The Bait of Satan*, has sold close to two million copies.

I would love to say I learned my lesson and never repeated such foolishness again. However, in my early forties I once again ignored God's clearly revealed will, as well as my wife's and a board member's strong counsel. This time the deception was stronger and the discipline of hardship, pain, and agony was even greater and lasted almost eighteen months. Once again I realized the idol I had created and repented, but not without the cost of much heartache.

I'm completely sure if Balaam would have embraced God's heart, he would have been much better off in the long run. However, he never truly turned away from his idolatry, and so he died under the judgment of God (see Joshua 13:22).

Dear one, I don't desire you to learn this the hard way as I did. I'm hopeful this strong message will cause you to avert the pain and hardship I unnecessarily lived through.

TAKE ACTION

If we will not submit our desires to God, they will lead us away from Him, and God may even deliver us over to them. Multiple times in Scripture we see that God had already made His will clear, yet when His people desired something contrary to it, He gave it to them, even when it brought them hardship.

God will still do this in our lives today. He will give us our desires even when they contradict His, but it will not lead to the blessing we wanted. It will lead to discipline that will be painful and unpleasant.

But we don't have to experience this. Instead we can trust God to do good for us. Often, He has a path laid out to give us the very things we desire, but in a righteous way. If we will follow Him, He will lead us in a blessed path, but the desired end will come in His time. Commit your way to the Lord today. Invite Him to lead you according to His desires and not your own. Ask Him what steps you can begin taking today to follow Him more closely. Write these down, and then do them.

17

MISGUIDED

To maintain our focus, let's briefly recap the heart of idolatry, which is when humanity, either believer or unbeliever, puts aside what God clearly reveals in order to satisfy cravings or desires contrary to His ways. For this reason, Paul states:

> For this you know, that no fornicator, unclean person, nor *covet-ous man, who is an idolater*, has any inheritance in the kingdom of Christ and God. Let no one deceive you with empty words, for because of these things the wrath of God comes upon the sons of disobedience. Therefore do not be partakers with them. (Ephesians 5:5–7 NKJV)

The wrath of God will come upon the unbeliever, but God also disciplines the believer who engages in idolatry (covetousness) in order to turn his or her back to His heart. However, if the believer stubbornly continues in disobedience, as did Balaam, the consequences can be as severe as death. Paul warns believers, "For if you live according to the flesh you will die" (Romans 8:13 NKJV). The apostle James also warns us, "When desire has conceived, it gives birth to sin; and sin, when it is full-grown, brings forth death. Do not be deceived, my beloved brethren" (James 1:15–16 NKJV).

Idolatry should be viewed as a slow-killing poison; it's spiritual kryptonite. We cannot afford to flirt with it. Idolatry's web is both subtle and strong—we got a glimpse of its power in looking at Balaam, but let's take it a step further. Read carefully God's warning to the leaders of Israel:

> The word of the Lord came to me, saying, "Son of man, these men have *set up their idols in their hearts,* and put before them that which causes them to stumble into iniquity. Should I let Myself be inquired of at all by them? (Ezekiel 14:2–3 NKJV)

Once again we clearly see idolatry not being limited to statues, altars, or temples. God leaves no room for doubt by clearly stating they had "set up their idols in their hearts." These aren't figurines under trees, in the city centers, or in temples. No, these were idols erected in their hearts. They were harboring desires that are contrary to God's will. God continues:

> "Therefore speak to them, and say to them, 'Thus says the Lord God: "Everyone of the house of Israel who sets up his idols in his heart, and puts before him what causes him to stumble into iniquity, and then comes to the prophet, I the Lord will answer him who comes, according to the multitude of his idols.""" (Ezekiel 14:4 NKJV)

When a person is entangled in idolatry (clinging to contrary desires) and comes before a minister requesting direction, counsel, or biblical teaching of any sort, he or she may get an answer, but it is not going to be according to God's will. It will be an answer similar to what Balaam received. *The New American Standard Bible* records the verse from Ezekiel like this: "I the Lord will be brought to give him an answer in the matter in view of the multitude of his idols."

Now hear the warning to the ministry leader who avoids confronting the idolatry of the seeker, but rather speaks to him or her as if all is well (prophets and priests were the ministry leaders in the Old Testament; from this point on I'll use relevant terms for today's ministry leaders):

> "But if the prophet does give the man the answer he desires [thus allowing himself to be a party to the inquirer's sin (idolatry)], I the Lord will see to it that the prophet is deceived in his answer." (Ezekiel 14:9 AMPC)

In prayer I've either wept or carried great sadness in pondering much of the teaching propagated by the modern ministry today, especially in the West. I've cried out for answers to what's behind the weak gospel messages being spoken and written. In answer, the Spirit of God led me to chapters 13 and 14 of Ezekiel. These chapters reveal what's behind the watered-down teachings that neglect to confront practiced sin: It's *idolatry*. If the minister presents an incomplete gospel because he doesn't want to lose followers or fame, it's nothing other than camouflaged covetousness. For this very reason in a time period when counterfeit ministry flourished, Jeremiah cries out:

> "Because from the least of them even to the greatest of them, everyone is given to covetousness. Prophets and priests and everyone in between twist words and doctor truth." (Jeremiah 6:13 NKJV, first sentence and MSG, second sentence)

I began to glimpse the deeper workings of the evident spiritual weakness—the kryptonite—in much of the modern church. I could see the discontentment of many professing believers, and from this heart condition has arisen desires for what's "lacking in life" (most often these are not authentic needs, but nothing more than wants or cravings).

The misguided leaders, also sidetracked by covetous desires, have proclaimed Scriptures that seemingly overlook and affirm the sinful life-style of seekers and at the same time conveniently avoid any Scriptures that would confront ungodly behavior. This idolatry opens up both minister and believer to receive messages or counsel that speaks directly to these wants or lusts and strengthens these desires or idols.

In the New Testament Paul prophesies, similar to Jeremiah and Ezekiel, of a future time period:

> For a time is coming when people will no longer listen to sound and wholesome teaching. They will follow *their own desires* and will look for teachers who will tell them whatever their itching ears want to hear. (2 Timothy 4:3)

Welcome to that time period! All that's necessary for seekers to hear what they want is to find "ministers" who are also in a state of covetousness.

On the other hand, a godly, God-fearing leader will not deviate from any of the counsel of God's Word. The Scripture in its entirety is adhered to, not select sections. This leader is not afraid to correct and confront, as well as to encourage.

These ministers Paul speaks of will be concerned with their reputation, appearance, growth, and agendas. They can be persuaded with the right outcome or reward, thus they will speak and teach in light of the hearer's desires, rather than faithfully declaring God's Word whether it is welcomed or not.

Only One Minister Declared Truth

Jehoshaphat, king of Judah, had allied himself with Ahab, king of Israel, through the marriage of their children. This was not a good move for Jehoshaphat, because he feared God, but Ahab was an idolater. After some time, Jehoshaphat went to Samaria to visit Israel's king.

Ahab petitioned Jehoshaphat to rally Judah to go to war alongside Israel and attack Syria. Jehoshaphat replied, "'Why, of course! You and I are brothers, and my troops are yours to command. We will certainly join you in battle.'" But then Jehoshaphat added, "'But first let's find out what the Lord says'" (see 2 Chronicles 18).

So King Ahab summoned four hundred of the most prominent ministers and leaders of Israel. These were *not* ministers of Baal, Asherah, Chemosh, or any other false god, but ministers of the Lord God (they spoke in the name of *Yahweh*). Ahab asked them if he should go to war or refrain.

The ministers all with one accord spoke, "Yes, go right ahead! God will give the king victory" (2 Chronicles 18:5). These leaders were trained to speak only positive and encouraging messages to hearers, especially important ones. Even though they were ministers of *Yahweh*, they were given to covetousness—they were idolaters.

Although these ministers were the most respected of Israel and their messages impressive, Jehoshaphat was not comfortable with this counsel. The fear of God in his life had kept his discernment intact. He asked, "Is there not still a prophet of the Lord here that we may inquire of Him?" (verse 6 NKJV). He knew these who spoke were prophets of *Yahweh*, but something wasn't right.

Ahab retorted, "'There is one more man who could consult the Lord for us, but I hate him, He never prophesies anything but trouble for me! His name is Micaiah'" (verse 7). To an idolater, or a community of believers who have become accustomed to flattery, a true minister of the gospel often seems negative and discouraging.

Micaiah was different than the others, because he didn't want a large following or anything from Ahab. He feared the Lord more than man and desired God's approval over success. He knew *Yahweh* was his source, and that he'd rather please Him than a king under kryptonite's influence. This kept him pure and free from the deception the other ministers operated in.

Ahab then sent for Micaiah. While they were waiting for the authentic man of God, the ministers continued to prophesy before the two kings. One of them, a Hebrew man named Zedekiah of the tribe of Benjamin, made horns of iron for himself and said, "This is what the Lord (*Yahweh*) says: With these horns you will gore the Arameans to death" (verse 10).

Then all the ministers counseled the king in unison, saying, "Go up to Ramoth-gilead and be victorious, for the Lord (*Yahweh*) will give the king victory" (verse 11). Surely there is safety in the multitude of leaders, right? And what was really encouraging and seemed safe was that the messages all agreed and were confirmation! Yes, they confirmed the exact *desires* of Ahab's heart and spoke directly to his desire for gain—idolatry!

Now while the ministers in one accord counseled the two kings, the messenger found Micaiah and spoke to him, saying, "'Now listen, the words of the prophets with one accord encourage the king. Therefore please let your word be like the word of one of them, and speak encouragement'" (2 Chronicles 18:12 NKJV).

I have heard similar words when invited to a few well-known churches. "John, encourage the people. Preach positive messages. Build them up and comfort them. We will end our service with an up-tempo song so can you end it on an upbeat note. We want them to leave feeling good." As if the mere messenger can tamper with the message of the King! If we tamper, we are now no longer ambassadors speaking as the oracles of God, but mere men using His positive words found in various places in the New Testament to bring forth what we desire.

Micaiah's response was blunt, because he couldn't be bought with flattery: "'As surely as the Lord lives, I will say only what my God says'" (verse 13).

Oh, Father, send us leaders who will do the same in our day!

When Micaiah came before Ahab, he was asked the same question already answered by the multitude of other ministers. "Micaiah replied sarcastically, 'Yes, go up and be victorious, for you will have victory over them!'" (verse 14).

Ahab became upset with Micaiah for mocking him. Micaiah then spoke God's word concerning the situation: "'In a vision I saw all Israel scattered on the mountains, like sheep without a shepherd. And the Lord said, "Their master has been killed. Send them home in peace"'" (verse 16).

Ahab turned to Jehoshaphat and said, "'Didn't I tell you? He never prophesies anything but trouble for me'" (verse 17).

Then Micaiah proceeded to tell Ahab what was really going on and what would actually happen:

"'Therefore hear the word of the Lord: I saw the Lord sitting on
His throne, and all the host of heaven standing on His right hand
and His left. And the Lord said, "Who will persuade Ahab king of
Israel to go up, that he may fall at Ramoth Gilead?" So one spoke
in this manner, and another spoke in that manner. Then a spirit
came forward and stood before the Lord, and said, "I will persuade
him." The Lord said to him, "In what way?" So he said, "I will go
out and be a lying spirit in the mouth of all his prophets." And the
Lord said, "You shall persuade him and also prevail; go out and do
so." Therefore look! The Lord has put a lying spirit in the mouth of
these prophets of yours, and the Lord has declared disaster against
you'" (verses 18–22 NKJV).

God answered Ahab according to the idolatry (covetousness) in his heart. The truth Ezekiel writes about is illustrated here. Not only does God speak directly to the idolatry in Balaam's heart, as seen in the last chapter and Ahab's in this chapter, but He does similarly with those who give the message.

Ahab received the message he wanted to hear, but he refused the true words of God that would have brought protection and deliverance. Ahab went out to battle. Even though he was protected in disguising himself so the Syrians wouldn't recognize him, he was struck by a wild arrow and died before day's end. You can hide from man, but you can never hide from God!

What about today? Do we desire the protection, provision, and deliverance God promises? Or do we desire to be flattered? Do we want to hear "peace" when in reality certain trouble looms from the deception we've bought into?

Can we just think it through in the light of Scripture? What's better—long-term protection in submitting to the entire counsel of God's word, or short-term superficial blessing while imminent discipline or judgment is just around the corner?

TAKE ACTION

Many professing Christians only want to hear words that make them feel good, and because of covetousness and the fear of man, many ministers are willing to only speak words that encourage their followers. In these cases, all the sweet words sound wonderful, but they are lacking and will lead both leaders and followers to an undesirable place.

We need to hear the truth, even if it hurts at first. No matter how painful it is to hear the truth, it is far less painful than the hardship we run toward when we live in deception.

You can be a person who pursues truth.

Start by asking God to speak His truth about your life, inviting Him to reveal any place where you have been unknowingly deceived. Write down the truths He tells you so you can meditate on them in the coming days and weeks. Then ask God to strengthen you to tell the truth, even if it's not what's popular or politically correct. You don't need to pick fights, but you are able to say, like Micaiah, "As surely as the Lord lives, I will say only what my God says."

18

A KNOCKOFF JESUS

Are you thinking, A *knockoff Jesus—what is that all about?* This chapter contains the subtle key element that draws believers into idolatry. Covering this aspect will help unlock the mystery of why so many in modern Christianity fall easy prey to spiritual kryptonite, which robs our strength as a church and as individuals.

Brought You to Myself

As I have mentioned before, Israel coming out of Egypt is symbolic of our salvation—our coming out of the world. Moses led the Israelites to Sinai, where he met God at the burning bush. Moses wanted his people to experience a similar encounter. Why would he want to lead them immediately to the Promised Land before introducing them to the Promiser? Once they arrived in Sinai, we read:

> Moses went up to God, and the Lord called to him from the mountain, saying, "Thus you shall say to the house of Jacob, and tell the children of Israel: 'You have seen what I did to the Egyptians, and

how I bore you on eagles' wings and *brought you to Myself.*'"
(Exodus 19:3–4 NKJV)

Look at His words, "brought you to Myself." This statement sums up the divine motivation behind our being saved from the world. God brought you to Himself. He desires you, He longs for your fellowship, and He wants a Father-child relationship.

Can you imagine how excited God was to meet these people who'd been in captivity for hundreds of years? I remember when Lisa was pregnant with each of our four sons. I couldn't wait for them to be born. I'd waited for nine long months. I wanted to hold them in my arms, watch them grow up, hear their voices, experience their personalities, and develop a father-son relationship with them. Simply put, I longed for them.

This was God's attitude, except He'd waited a lot longer than nine months!

The people needed to make certain preparations for a successful meeting. God said, "'Prepare the people for my arrival. Consecrate them today and tomorrow, and have them wash their clothing. Be sure they are ready on the third day, for on that day the Lord will come down on Mount Sinai as all the people watch'" (Exodus 19:10–11).

The Lord was telling His people, "I long for you, but for us to have an authentic encounter, you must wash the filth of Egypt off your clothing. I'm your Father, but I also am a holy God and will not have a superficial relationship with you."

It's impossible to have a deep, meaningful relationship with others who are selfish. God has given Himself fully to us; He cannot have us doing what the world does, using those we have relationships with to satisfy our own desires or ego.

In Sinai, two days passed and on the beginning of the third day, the Lord came down to introduce Himself. When He did, the people backed away and trembled with fear. They said to Moses, "'You speak to us, and we will listen. But don't let God speak directly to us, or we will die'" (Exodus 20:19).

Moses was distraught. How could they draw away from the One who had saved and rescued them from bondage? How could they not want to hear their Creator's voice? But can you imagine God's disappointment? He'd longed for this moment. He yearned to know them the way He was getting to know Moses. Yet they rejected His presence.

I can't imagine how I would feel if one of my sons said to me, "Dad, I just don't want you to speak to me directly. I only want to hear your messages through one of my brothers." How devastating!

A Priesthood Established

God determined a priesthood would have to be established since the people didn't want direct interaction with Him. A priest is someone who speaks to God for the people. The Jews already had a prophet, Moses, who was speaking from God to the people. However, God would have to establish a priesthood to maintain a similitude of ongoing fellowship with the people.

God then said, "'Go down and bring Aaron back up with you'" (Exodus 19:24). Aaron would become His first priest, however, this was not God's original plan. Initially He wanted all of them to be priests. When they first arrived at Sinai, He said, ""You will be my kingdom of priests, my holy nation." This is the message you must give to the people of Israel'" (Exodus 19:6). He wanted everyone in Israel to have the ability to communicate with Him.

God instructed Moses to bring Aaron back up the mountain with him. However, we have no record of Aaron making it to the summit. For some reason, he ends up back down in the camp with the people, and Moses ends up on the mountaintop for forty days and nights. Why did Aaron not go? Did he find more comfort in the presence of people rather than God? Was he more afraid of being alone with God? We don't know the answer, but we do know what Aaron was about to do is nothing short of mind-blowing.

A Knockoff Yahweh

When the people saw how long it was taking Moses to come back down the mountain, they gathered around Aaron. (Exodus 32:1)

What's going on? First, the people had desires of what they wanted fulfilled, and they needed a man of God to accommodate them. Second, Aaron had a leadership gift on his life, and this gift attracts people. This is an important point, because people are drawn to a strong leader, whether the leader's obeying God or not. Just because a leader draws a significant following doesn't necessarily mean he is in sync with God. Hear what the people say to Aaron:

"Come, make us gods that shall go before us; for *as for* this Moses, the man who brought us up out of the land of Egypt, we do not know what has become of him." (Exodus 32:1 NKJV)

The first thing to notice is that the people do not say, "As for God, we do not know what's become of Him." This is an important point we'll discuss shortly.

Second, notice that they say, "make us gods." The Hebrew word for *gods* is *elohiym*. This word is found slightly more than 2,600 times in the Old Testament. Over 2,250 times, this word refers to God Almighty. For example, it appears thirty-two times alone in the first chapter of Genesis. The very first verse of the Bible reads, "In the beginning *elohiym* created the heavens and the earth."

Another example would be Deuteronomy 13:4: "'You shall walk after the Lord (*Yahweh*) your God (*elohiym*) and fear Him, and keep His commandments and obey His voice; you shall serve Him and hold fast to Him'" (NKJV). You can see in this Scripture the Lord's name is given, "Yahweh," and then He's referred to as our *elohiym*. He is God, the absolute authority and ultimate source.

However, slightly over 250 times in the Old Testament, *elohiym* is used to depict a false god, such as Dagon (1 Samuel 5:7) or Baal (1 Kings 18:21). So we must always read this word in context to know who is being spoken of.

Aaron responds to the people's request by requesting gold from their earrings. He melts the gold and then fashions the infamous calf. Once completed, the people say, "'This *is* your *god*, O Israel, that brought you out of the land of Egypt!'" (Exodus 32:4 NKJV). The Hebrew word for *god* is again *elohiym*. However, we are beginning to get a clue as to who is being spoken of here from their words, "that brought you out of the land of Egypt." They knew who had brought them out—they weren't stupid. Our clue is confirmed, however, in the very next verse:

> So when Aaron saw *it,* he built an altar before it. And Aaron made a proclamation and said, "Tomorrow *is* a feast to the LORD." (Exodus 32:5 NKJV)

The word "Lord" in this verse is *Yahweh*. The CWSB states:

> The word refers to the proper name of the God of Israel, particularly the name by which He revealed Himself to Moses (Exodus 6:2, 3). The divine name has traditionally not been pronounced, primarily out of respect for its sacredness. Until the Renaissance, it was written without vowels in the Hebrew text of the Old Testament, being rendered as *YHWH*.

This word, except in this reference, is never used to refer to or name a false god in the entire Bible. There is no mistaking what is going on. Almost beyond belief, Aaron and the people look right at that calf and call it *Yahweh*. They don't call this calf Baal, Dagon, Asherah, Ra, Nephthys, or any other Egyptian god's name. They don't say, "Behold Ra, who delivered us out of Egypt."

Recall that they had said, "We don't know what's become of Moses." They hadn't said, "We don't know what's become of God." They are not denying *Yahweh's* existence or involvement in their lives. They still acknowledge it was Jehovah (or *Yahweh*) that saved them, delivered them, healed them, and provided for them. They just have changed His true image into their manageable image of *Yahweh* who will give them what they want.

Here's a contemporary example of what this looks like: Lisa and I travel extensively and we have an excellent team at our ministry, Messenger International. So what I'm about to write is strictly hypothetical, because our team members would never do this. As leaders, there are several operational and cultural principles that Lisa and I consistently stress, because they are important to us. A few of them are: We ask our team for nine hours of productivity in eight hours. We want a fun work environment, to do everything with excellence, to love and serve any person, partner, or leader who contacts us, to meet certain daily and weekly quotas, and the list continues. Our Chief Operations Officer (COO), who I will give the fictional name of Tim, is responsible to make sure the operational and cultural standards we've asked for are maintained.

Let's assume Lisa and I are on the road, but not only both of us, but also our COO is away. The next one in charge would be our Chief Financial Officer (CFO), Jordan (also fictional). Once Tim leaves, soon afterward Jordan declares to the team, "Hey team, John and Lisa want us to have a fun atmosphere. Let's hire a DJ and set up a dance floor with some smoke and lights, and let's party for the next few days."

The entire time the party is going on, the team "confesses" that they are doing exactly what we've asked of them. They repeatedly acknowledge us saying, "This is John and Lisa's desire; they want us to have a fun environment." Then one of the team members shouts out, "Hey! I have John on the phone. I'm telling him about our party; he's so pleased with us." That of course would be a lie, because if I were on the phone and knew what was going on, I would be very angry with my team.

Let's now say that our COO returns to the office before either Lisa or I do. He also would be very upset. He'd turn off the music, send back the lights and smoke machine, and let our team have it. "This is not what John and Lisa want," he would say. "You have misrepresented them!" Then he would fire the ringleaders who'd created the counterfeit culture.

Now look at Israel's behavior after creating this manageable *"Yahweh"*:

> Then they rose early on the next day, offered burnt offerings, and
> brought peace offerings; and the people sat down to eat and drink,
> and rose up to play. (Exodus 32:6 NKJV)

This is the feast day to *Yahweh*. The leaders and people bring offerings to Him, then they let loose. They have all convinced themselves that they are doing what their *"Yahweh"* is OK with or pleased with. They believe He has no problems with their gluttony, partying, and revelry (which we can imagine included sexual immorality). They have ascribed behavior to be acceptable to God (*Yahweh*) that isn't pleasing to Him at all.

They have now entered into the most deceptive form of idolatry. They have created a knockoff *Yahweh*, one different than who He really is. This now gives them permission to live however they desire and do it with His approval. This is foundationally no different than the pagan nations who refused to worship (obey) God. Again Paul says, "They began to think up foolish ideas of what God was like" (Romans 1:21). The only difference is that the pagan nations call their gods names like Dagon, Baal, Hapi, Ammit, Sopdu, and so forth, while Israel called their deity *Yahweh*.

God then says to the COO, Moses, "'Quick! Go down the mountain! Your people whom you brought from the land of Egypt have corrupted themselves. How quickly they have turned away from the way I commanded them to live!'" (Exodus 32:7–8).

Moses returned, and there was some accounting for to accomplish. First for Aaron, the one left in charge, then the leaders, and finally the people. We read, "Moses saw that Aaron had let the people get completely out of control, much to the amusement of their enemies. So he stood at the entrance to the camp and shouted, 'All of you who are on the LORD's side, come here and join me'" (Exodus 32:25–26). They, as well as we, don't take sides with the Lord by simply professing His name or singing songs to Him. We choose His side by choosing to live according to what He declares.

This brings us to several very important questions:

In present times, have we created a "Jesus" who will give us whatever our misled passions desire?

Are we acknowledging that He shed His blood for us, saved us, and delivered us from the world?

Are we singing songs to and about Him and that He's made heaven available to us, but in truth "our Jesus" is not the actual Jesus seated at the right hand of the Father?

Have we created a knockoff Jesus?

Are numerous people in the church deceived, as were these Israelites who came out of Egypt?

And an additional question: Who are the COOs like Moses who are going to come down from the mountain of God and confront the deceived with a heart full of fire and love?

If they don't arise, our deception will only grow stronger. And kryptonite will continue to exploit our weakness, even to the point of death.

It's easy in the Western world to say you believe in Jesus. Much of the West, however, is jaded against Christianity because there's little difference between Christians and the world. Christians proclaim the name of Jesus and then say they honor God while living a sinful life that He clearly disapproves of. As Moses declared when he called Israel to account, "Whoever is on the Lord's side, come to me!" It is time for true Christians to arise and call their brothers and sisters to come into the truth.

Following Jesus costs us everything. Our lives are not our own. Our will is submitted to God, or He isn't truly our Lord. Our faith is in Him to provide all we need. This is the call of Christianity—yes, come be saved, but you must die to your old self and become new.

Reflect on the true calling of Christianity. Write down your thoughts of how this is the same as or different from what you have been taught. Then find someone in your family or church to talk about this with. Give this truth to them.

19

THE STARTING
PLACE

It's evident that when Moses descends from the mountain of God, Israel is into full-blown idolatry, even though they still acknowledge it is *Yahweh* who saved and delivered them from Egypt. As we discussed, idolatry is rooted in disobeying what God has clearly revealed to us. If we confess Jesus Christ as our Lord and Savior but are clearly disobedient to His authority, that becomes the most deceptive form of idolatry.

Let's return to the hypothetical example of our team at Messenger International. Once our COO, Tim, comes back to our office and sees the unruly partying, he would be furious with our CFO, Jordan. However, Jordan could easily say to Tim, "But we are doing exactly what John and Lisa asked us to do! We created a fun environment!"

How would Tim respond? "Yes, John and Lisa do want a fun environment, but what about all the other directives they've given us—nine hours' worth of work from an eight-hour day, availability to any person who contacts us, meeting daily quotas, and all the rest? You've isolated and focused on one aspect of what they've asked for and neglected all their other instructions."

Have we done something like this in the modern church? I believe we have found certain instructions in the New Testament that appeal to us. We have proclaimed that we are saved by grace through faith, and we cannot earn this grace because it is God's favor. We have stressed loving one another, enjoying life, serving one another, singing new songs of praise and worship, being relevant, executing good leadership, and creating a healthy community. We proclaim all of this with fervent passion. These are all good practices and all are supported by the New Testament.

However, are we neglecting the importance of meekness, holiness, sexual purity, and abstinence from other sins, such as pornography?

Have we warned those we love to flee homosexuality, fornication, drunkenness, crude jokes, empty foolish talking, unforgiveness, bitterness, gossip, and many other important commandments, instructions, and warnings found in the New Testament?

Can we solely focus on the aspects of Jesus's words that don't collide with our society's established standards and perversions?

Can we create a Jesus that doesn't confront the ungodly ways of our culture?

Can we avoid addressing what He hates, and only proclaim His words that society deems admirable?

Can we widen the road and gate that leads to life?

Can we believe that if a person just recites a few magical words, they are automatically saved?

Have we created a knockoff Jesus, different from the One revealed by the entire counsel of Scripture, and are we purposefully ignoring the challenging issues of the New Testament? Paul makes a statement that none of us should ignore:

"I declare today that I have been faithful. If anyone suffers eternal death, it's not my fault, for I didn't shrink from *declaring all* that God wants you to know." (Acts 20:26–27)

Paul didn't speak only the pleasant words of the gospel, but he was sure to *declare all* God wants us to know. He wasn't like our CFO who only told our team the fun aspect of Lisa's and my desires. Paul's words in the NKJV read, "'I have not shunned to declare to you *the whole counsel* of God.'" The *Amplified Classic* reads, "'I never shrank or kept back or fell short from declaring to you the whole purpose and plan and counsel of God.'"

If we avoid sharing the uncomfortable teachings of the New Testament, we can't say like Paul, "If anyone suffers eternal death, it's not my fault." In fact, might the converse be true if we withhold key portions of the New Testament? It was in our power to share the whole truth, but we avoided it. Were we concerned that seekers wouldn't desire to return to our next service, gathering, or small group meeting?

Now that we've gone years in our Christian culture avoiding important character issues addressed in Scripture, we are reaping the harvest of our neglect. Sadly, many are on a wayward path. Countless examples could be given in regard to this point. One that comes to mind is a very influential minister, a widely read author, and popular conference speaker. In 2016, she declared her marriage was complete (whatever that means). She divorced her husband and, at the time of this writing, is living with and engaged to a female.

She regularly reports to her followers of their life together. In one post, she shares a photo of being affectionately kissed by her female partner and comments how her life journey has led her to this relationship and that every bit of it is "holy." That's not how Scripture would describe it. My heart is broken for her. Here is a "minister of the gospel" who really believes she is right with God and has a desire to help, serve, and love people, but she is genuinely deceived.

What's even more disconcerting are the countless supportive and favorable comments made by her hundreds of thousands of followers. Her posts indicate she's representing God and her followers agree. Through this entire journey her popularity has grown, not diminished. This is heartrending, painful, tragic, and fear-inducing all at the same time.

In another tragic situation, one of the most well-known evangelical leaders in America has recently announced to all his followers and the church at large that we should fully accept homosexual couples as genuine followers of Jesus. He said that his decision has come from spending a lot of time with homosexual couples and discovering their relationship works much the same as a man and wife. The only possibility of reaching this conclusion is to willingly eliminate Scriptures in the New Testament and ignore the entire biblical narrative. As in the case of Aaron and the golden calf, multitudes will be swayed away from truth by this leader's announcement.

This is tragic deception. Due to the knockoff Jesus that has evolved from our Western philosophy of ministry, the authentic Savior is increasingly difficult for lost people to find. We must ask, "Is this the real Jesus? Is this the love of God? Is genuine love solely defined by only kindness, patience, and giving to others?" All of these attributes are true and also popular with our society. However, can we just ignore how love is definitively defined in Scripture: "This is the love of God, that we keep His commandments" (1 John 5:3 NKJV)?

Have we settled for only a partial counsel of the New Testament to find our definition of love?

The Necessity to Repent

Is this wayward gospel a result of the absence of repentance? Was the female minister-author, the pastor, and the many others ever told to walk away from sin in order to follow Jesus? Or were they told to simply pray what has become our standard prayer: "Jesus, come into my life and make me a Christian"?

Listen to Paul's words:

I never shrank back from telling you what you needed to hear,
either publicly or in your homes. I have had one message for Jews
and Greeks alike—the *necessity* of repenting from sin and turning
to God, and of having faith in our Lord Jesus. (Acts 20:20–21)

Only one message! The first step is the *necessity* of repenting from
sin! Repentance is *mandatory* to become a child of God, not optional.
Yet it's often not mentioned in our typical explanation and invitation to
salvation.

A few years ago on the first day of a fast, I heard the Holy Spirit say,
"Read Mark chapter one." I eagerly read the entire chapter and didn't get
any different insight than in times past. The Holy Spirit said, "Read it
again." I read it, still nothing new. He said the same words a third, fourth,
and fifth time. I read it again several times . . . still nothing. This went on
approximately seven times. Finally, I read at a snail's pace, and this time
the opening statement jumped off the page:

"The beginning of the gospel of Jesus Christ . . ." (Mark 1:1 NKJV)

The next words were the key, ". . . Behold, I send My messenger before
Your face, who will prepare Your way before You." The messenger was
John the Baptist. His ministry was one of a "baptism of repentance." Baptism means full immersion, not partial. John's message of full repentance
is the beginning, or starting place, of the gospel. No one can come into a
genuine relationship with Jesus without starting with genuine repentance.

The Holy Spirit then spoke to me, "John's ministry is at the very beginning of every one of the gospels. John's story is not in a book in the
Old Testament, because his message is a vital part of the New Testament
gospel."

Next the Spirit led me over to Jesus's words:

"For all the prophets and the law prophesied until John." (Matthew 11:13 NKJV)

I jumped up from my seat and shouted, "Wow, that's right!" Jesus didn't say, "For all the prophets and the law prophesied until Me (Jesus Christ)." No, because John's message of complete repentance is the starting place of the New Testament gospel. You haven't entered a relationship with Jesus unless you've fully repented of known patterns of sin.

Repentance is the front door!

Recall our story of Justin and Angela and her strange idea of marriage. She never gave up her old boyfriends. She deeply loved Justin, he was her favorite, and she planned to spend most of her time with him. However, she was never informed that in order to enter a marriage covenant with Justin, it would be *necessary* to cut ties—mentally, emotionally, and physically—with all her old boyfriends. This decision would be the *starting place* or *beginning* of her ability to enter into a covenant with Justin.

She was shocked that he was angry about her plans to go out with Tony. *Why is he so upset?* She kept thinking, *Is he jealous?* Yes, he was very jealous, and he should be. God is jealous for us, and it is only right that He is. We've entered into covenant with Him—how can we bring other lovers into it?

Is it coincidental that John's first words in Scripture are, *"Repent,* for the kingdom of heaven is at hand!"* (Matthew 3:2 NKJV)?

Is John the only one saying this? Is his message isolated, not spoken by other New Testament messengers? No way! Jesus's first instructions are:

"Repent, for the kingdom of heaven is at hand." (Matthew 4:17 NKJV)

Our Lord and King knew repentance is the necessary and critical step to having a lasting relationship with God. Amazingly, this is the criteria He used to determine whether or not people belonged to God.

Then Jesus began to denounce the towns where he had done so many of his miracles, because they hadn't *repented of their sins* and turned to God (see Matthew 11:20).

If all a person has to do to be saved is "turn to God," then that's all Jesus would have pointed out. However, just as Angela had to forsake old boyfriends in order to give herself fully to Justin, so we must repent of our sins in order to give ourselves to Jesus.

We see this message repeatedly, because it is the core mission of Jesus's ministry. He declares, "'I have come to call . . . those who know they are sinners and *need to repent*'" (Luke 5:32). Consider the word "*need*." Repentance is not optional. Jesus also made this statement to a group of people: "'You will perish, too, unless you *repent of your sins* and turn to God'" (Luke 13:3).

Here's the truth: *There is no turning to God without repentance.*

Let's move on to see how Jesus's disciples viewed sharing the gospel. This is what they declared on their first solo mission assignment: "So the disciples went out, telling everyone they met to *repent of their sins* and turn to God" (Mark 6:12).

Consider the words, *everyone they met*. Since there's no salvation without repentance, it's necessary that you have to tell everyone! Even the rich man who was burning in hell knew the importance of repenting of sins:

"The rich man replied, 'No, Father Abraham! But if someone is sent to them from the dead, then they will *repent of their sins* and turn to God.'" (Luke 16:30)

What about after the resurrection? Did the message change? Luke records Jesus appearing to His disciples. He rebukes them for their hardness of heart and then opens their understanding. He then recites what the prophets foretold of Him:

> "It was also written that this message would be proclaimed in the authority of his name to all the nations, beginning in Jerusalem: 'There is forgiveness of sins for *all who repent*.'" (Luke 24:47)

The prophets foretold forgiveness could only be found in the Savior if there is first repentance, and the apostle Peter follows suit. Hear his first words instructing eager seekers how to be saved on the day of Pentecost:

> "Each of you must *repent of your sins* and turn to God, and be baptized in the name of Jesus Christ for the forgiveness of your sins." (Acts 2:38)

Again, there's no turning to God without first repenting. How about Paul? Did he alter his message for the Gentiles? Not at all:

> I obeyed that vision from heaven. I preached first to those in Damascus, then in Jerusalem and throughout all Judea, and also to the *Gentiles*, that all *must repent of their sins* and turn to God—and prove they have changed by the good things they do. (Acts 26:19–20)

Look at the words, "all must," not "should," nor "it's a good idea." Not a chance! What he says is "all must repent of their sins."

Paul explained how God Himself gave this as a requirement for anyone, either Jew or Gentile, to come to salvation:

> "God overlooked people's ignorance about these things in earlier times, but now He commands everyone everywhere to *repent of their sins* and turn to Him." (Acts 17:30)

If you look at the foundational teachings of Jesus Christ, to no surprise, the very first on the list is, guess what?

> So let us stop going over the *basic teachings* about Christ again
> and again. Let us go on instead and become mature in our under-
> standing. Surely we don't need to start again with the fundamental
> importance of *repenting from evil deeds* and placing our faith in
> God. (Hebrews 6:1)

I've not covered all the locations in the New Testament where this command is issued, but I've listed enough of them to show the importance of repentance from sin. There is no placing faith in our Lord Jesus Christ unless there is first repentance from known disobedience to God.

So we cannot become a Christian if we are willfully hanging on to pornography.

We cannot become a believer if we refuse to stop having sex with our girlfriend or boyfriend.

We cannot become a Christian if we refuse to turn away from homosexuality.

We cannot become a believer if we refuse to abstain from cheating on our taxes.

We cannot become a follower of Jesus if we cling to gender perversion.

We cannot become a Christian if we refuse to walk away from unforgiveness. And this list is far from exhaustive.

If we insist on clinging to limited parts of what the New Testament commands, then we have created a "knockoff Jesus." We are deceived in our heart and our faith is only imaginative. And we are warned, "Don't just listen to God's word. You must do what it says. Otherwise, you are only fooling yourselves" (James 1:22).

How are seekers to know this unless we proclaim it? As leaders, do we just assume they'll figure this out? If our only appeal to seekers is, "Are you away from God? He's waiting for you to come home. Just pray this prayer with me"—is that truly loving them?

If this is our approach, we are doing what Angela's family or others did in instructing her about marriage. They neglected to inform her that in order to be married to Justin, she had to walk away from her old boyfriends. Had they assumed she'd eventually figure it out? Now Angela's confused and bewildered. And Justin, the one who loves her and is truly committed to their covenant, is quite angry.

No matter the audience, there is only one true gospel that must be presented like this: first, *repentance* from all known sin and then turning to God. There's no true believing unless there's first *repentance*.

The contemporary mode of communicating the gospel is to get seekers to believe and pray, then turn from known sin—a few weeks, months, or even years down the line. But is it possible that there'll be no motivation later to repent, because the seekers will believe they're already saved?

Angela regretted not being told the truth before she made the decision to marry Justin. We, too, only develop conflicted church attenders when we don't tell them the truth about what's required to be saved.

TAKE ACTION

The New Testament presents a clear message: There is no salvation without repentance from sin. You cannot marry Jesus while still in relationship with the world. You have to die to your old life in order to begin your new one.

If you spend any time as a communicator, you learn quickly you need to make your most important points crystal clear. If you don't, your audience will likely misunderstand you, and the purpose of your communication will be lost. God knows this. That's why He has made this so clear—we must repent!

By now, you have probably repented several times while reading this book, but how does this chapter reinforce just how important repentance is? What difference does it make in your life now that you know this? How does it change the way you interact with the world, your loved ones, or with the lost? Ask God to show you one specific action you can introduce into your life in response to how important it is to repent. As always, write down what He tells you, including your plan for how you will fulfill those actions.

20

REPENTANCE

In the previous chapter, we repeatedly heard from Scripture, "Repent of your sins and turn to God." Since repentance isn't optional, but *necessary* to receive eternal life, let's discuss it in more detail. In unpacking this truth, we will also discover (in a future chapter) that as Christians, *repentance* is essential to maintain intimate fellowship with God.

First, it is crucial to understand that repentance in the New Testament is different from repentance in the Old Testament. While repenting, God's people in the Old Testament would wear sackcloth and ashes. They would wail, fall to the ground, and often shed many tears to show their repentance. It was an outward display of remorse and a return to godly obedience. We will discover in the New Testament, however, that the emphasis isn't found in our outward display, but centers upon the heart.

New Testament Repentance

In the New Testament, the noun "repentance" (*metanoia*) and the verb "repent" (*metanoeō*) are found twenty-four and thirty-four times, respectively. The most common and widely accepted definition is "a change of mind." However, if we leave it simply at that, we lose the strength of its true definition.

The *Baker Encyclopedia of the Bible* states that repentance is "literally a change of mind, not about individual plans, intentions, or beliefs, but rather a change in the *whole personality* from a sinful course of action to God" (emphasis added).

I love the words *whole personality*. I can change my mind, yet not be fully persuaded. In using these words, the scholars show there is more to it than simply a change of the mind or intellect. *The Lexham Theological Wordbook* goes deeper by stating that repentance is "a process in which the individual reorients the mind and will—away from sin and toward God."

Repentance certainly involves the mind but goes deeper; it involves our will and our emotions. It penetrates to the depth of our heart where we are firmly persuaded from the core of our being. Jesus says:

> "For *from the heart* come evil thoughts, murder, adultery, all sexual immorality, theft, lying, and slander. These are what defile you."
> (Matthew 15:19–20)

Behavior, whether spontaneous or habitual, originates from our innermost parts. If all that is necessary for true repentance is to solely change our intellect, then Jesus would have said these behaviors come from our mind. Scripture states, "For as he thinks in his heart, so is he" (Proverbs 23:7 NKJV). The way we perceive life deep inside dictates our actions or responses, and these define us.

You may be thinking, *I don't want to be defined by my behavior*. I agree, it's not a pleasant truth, but we can't ignore Jesus's words: "'You can identify them by their fruit, that is, by the way they act'" (Matthew 7:16). The truth is we are defined by our actions, not by our intentions.

This knowledge alone illustrates the power of the gospel, for it contains the ability to change these innermost thoughts, thereby altering our conduct. To be truly impacted by the gospel isn't a new way of thinking or an emotionally charged response, but a deep change of perception and belief accompanied by genuinely reformed behavior.

Repentance occurs when we awaken to the truth and are fully persuaded to the core of our being that our philosophy or behavior is contrary to our Creator's. This heartfelt realization results not only in a change of view, but in our desires and conduct as well. What we desire and love that's contrary to God, we firmly decide to change in our deepest parts, to walk away from these things—even to hate them. Repentance is true humility, and humility opens the door for God's unmerited grace, which enables us to live godly lives.

The Unbeliever

Repentance applies to both the unbeliever and the believer, but in slightly different ways. Let's address the unbeliever first.

In the previous chapter, we consistently heard from John the Baptist, Jesus, and His disciples, "Repent from sin and turn to God." These two commands are actually closely connected and are not independent of each other. In other words, you cannot have one without the other, because they are like different sides of the same coin. Biblical repentance is to turn to God in all aspects. The one who truly comes to Christ declares:

> "I've lived as the one who judges what is best for me, but now I know I'm completely wrong. From this moment forward, no matter what God says is best, I will believe and embrace it with all my heart, mind, and behavior."

This person decides from the heart (which includes intellect, emotions, and will) to do His will. The accompanied blessing is he or she will continue to hear the voice of God. Again, as a reminder, Jesus states, "'Anyone who wants (*wills*) to do the will of God will know whether my teaching is from God'" (John 7:17). In repenting, the unbeliever turns from self-governance to absolute submission to God, and this opens their heart to hear His voice.

When unbelievers truly repent, they walk away from idolatry and take a posture of complete submission and obedience to God's authority. In essence they declare, "No longer will I embrace thoughts, beliefs, reasonings, or arguments that exalt themselves above God's Word." Paul boldly declares:

> We use God's mighty weapons, not worldly weapons, to *knock down* the strongholds of human reasoning and to *destroy* false arguments. We *destroy* every proud obstacle that keeps people from knowing God. We capture their rebellious thoughts and teach them to obey Christ. (2 Corinthians 10:4–5)

God's weapons are His Word, wisdom, and counsel. Worldly weapons are society's philosophy, culture, customs, laws, or lifestyles that are contrary to God's Word. You may question, "The world has weapons?" Oh yes, there is a continual onslaught of hell via the world's system to compromise the Christian and unbeliever alike.

In the above Scripture, notice the terms "knock down" and "destroy." These exact words are used frequently in the Old Testament when people turned away from idolatry. Israel would *knock down,* smash, demolish, or *destroy* erected idols. (Keep in mind what they were actually doing; the root of idolatry is habitual patterns of known sin. This is what they were really destroying, not just statues.)

This principle Paul speaks of is no different. We use the Word of God to confront these idolatrous thoughts in men and women who are estranged from Christ. In doing so, the hearers repent of (knock down and destroy) all human reasonings, arguments, or disobedience to God's authority. In essence, this is what it means to repent of practiced sin. In so doing, a person is actually turning to God, thereby making him or her free.

Philosophical Difference

This brings us to one of the huge philosophical differences of ministry in modern times, especially in the West. A vast number of leaders have adopted the mindset that in order to reach the lost, we need to focus our messages on the non-confrontational aspects of the gospel. In other words, stay positive and refrain from identifying sins that require repentance. With such an approach, either knowingly or unknowingly, we become like a salesperson who attempts to persuade the buyer of the item's benefits, neglecting to mention any downsides. Sadly, this mindset has become almost standard in methods to reach the lost.

There are two apparent benefits to this errant philosophy of ministry. The first being, we eliminate any chance of beating people up. Legalism does lack compassion, which is more focused on the letter of the law due to the desire of some to be right, to control behavior, and to be the recognized authority. Due to its harshness, legalism leaves in its wake wounded souls who now have no place to seek God since the individual or institution that represented Jesus has beat them up. Legalism could be the cause of more people turning away from a true relationship with God than anything else.

Jesus identified the consequences of legalistic "ministry": "'For you shut the door of the Kingdom of Heaven in people's faces. You won't go in yourselves, and you don't let others enter either'" (Matthew 23:13).

So our desire to eliminate legalism is correct, but we can't swing the pendulum to the complete other side of the spectrum. Should we avoid true New Testament ministry for fear of sliding back in to what once damaged people? Do we dodge confronting sin and calling for repentance to avoid any possible hint of legalism? Do we throw the baby out with the dirty bathwater?

We have to address these questions, because what has now become the norm in evangelism is no longer scriptural. How can we offer salvation without any repentance if the Bible clearly shows repentance is *necessary*? And are those we are reaching with such a limited gospel truly being saved?

The second "benefit" of sidestepping repentance is that we can win converts more easily and thus build a much larger ministry, church, or small group. But have we forgotten that it was the majority who followed Aaron's error? The largeness or smallness of our following doesn't determine if we are in alignment with God's heart. Truth, not numbers, is the determining factor.

Have we forgotten the price to follow Jesus? Have we overlooked His repeated instructions to forsake sin (deny ourselves) and take up our cross (complete willingness to obey Him)?

If we don't confront practiced sin, the person who receives Jesus will continue to live by the standards set by our society, rather than the Word of God. In our society, it is perfectly normal to live and sleep with your unmarried lover, to practice homosexuality, even to the point of what's incorrectly labeled as *marriage;* to drink in excess; to get high on marijuana and other substances; to entertain ourselves with lewd, irreverent, or corrupt programs, videos, or movies; and more—my list is far from complete. Yet all these behaviors directly oppose New Testament commandments.

Heaven's Standards

Really, are there commandments in the New Testament? Oh yes, in fact there are over five hundred commands in the New Testament to depart from various thoughts or behaviors. The apostle Paul, the man who re-

would cling to their chairs and fall out of their pews, screaming and crying out their repentance, pleading with God for salvation. It was these who repented—by the thousands upon thousands—who changed the world. Entire cities turned from sin to God.

Preaching repentance might empty our churches or more likely, it just might fill them. Ask God to show you the potential of repentance, and then pray for Him to release that in your life and in your church.

21

THE THREE KINGS

A rereading of six books in the Old Testament is what inspired the writing of this book.

Over the last forty years, I've read and studied the books of Samuel, Kings, and Chronicles on many occasions. But recently, I methodically prayed and read through them like never before. I was amazed when God opened my eyes to something I had not previously noticed.

What follows may seem a bit academic and even tedious, but to only state the conclusion of what I discovered will diminish the impact if I don't share the brief synopses of the kings of the Old Testament. There is a powerful truth that is revealed by summarizing their lives that is not as obvious if the six books are read in their entirety—due to all the storylines woven into them.

In all my previous reading of these books, I'd always assumed there were two basic categories of kings—those who "did what was right in the sight of the Lord" and those who were "idolaters." However, I have since realized there were actually *three* groups of kings.

The truth is that none of the kings of Israel truly did what was right in the Lord's sight, with the exception of Jehu, but sadly even he also went wayward toward the end of his life. So let's turn to Judah. There were a total of twenty kings who ruled over Judah, other than Saul, David, and Solomon. The idolatrous kings were Rehoboam, Abijam, Joram, Ahaziah, Athaliah (queen), Ahaz, Manasseh, Amon, Jehoahaz, Jehoiakim, Jehoiachin, and Zedekiah. Under these kings' leadership, Judah suffered unique difficulties and attacks from their adversaries, which often could not be overcome and did a great deal of damage to the nation.

Then there were the kings who did what was right. (David and Solomon did what was right, although Solomon faltered in his later years.) After the kingdom split, they were: Asa, Jehoshaphat, Joash, Amaziah, Uzziah, Jotham, Hezekiah, and Josiah. However, this list of eight kings can be broken down into two further categories. The first are those who did what was right in the sight of the Lord in their personal lives, but they didn't address and tear down the high places of idol worship among the people they led.

Conversely, in the second group were those who not only did what was right in the sight of the Lord in their personal lives, but also tore down and destroyed the high places of idol worship among those they led. The success of the nation under these kings was considerably different than those who didn't confront the high places. Let's look at each one of them.

1. David. There was no idolatry in the nation during his reign. He passionately encouraged the people to serve the Lord with all their heart, mind, soul, and body. He didn't lose wars, and his kingdom became very wealthy. He positioned his son well to begin his reign.

2. Solomon. For a good portion of Solomon's reign, he followed the footsteps of his father David. The results of his obedience, not only in his life but among those he led, were nothing short of remarkable. We read, "During the lifetime of Solomon, all of Judah and Israel lived in peace and safety. And from Dan in the north to Beersheba in the south, each family had its own home

and garden" (1 Kings 4:25). Ponder this: No one needed govern-ment assistance, because prosperity abounded in the nation. His leadership was so great that "kings from every nation sent their ambassadors to listen to the wisdom of Solomon" (1 Kings 4:34). In fact, later we read, "People from every nation came to con-sult him and to hear the wisdom God had given him" (1 Kings 10:24). We also read, "He succeeded in everything, and all Israel obeyed him" (1 Chronicles 29:23). The nation was extremely successful: "The king made silver and gold as plentiful in Jerusa-lem as stone. And valuable cedar timber was as common as the sycamore-fig trees that grow in the foothills of Judah" (2 Chroni-cles 1:15).

However, as time passed Solomon disobeyed God and mar-ried many foreign women. They turned his heart toward other gods (known practiced sin) and consequently, the Lord raised up adversaries who hindered Solomon's progress and started trouble for the kingdom (see 1 Kings 11:14, 23). The result of his known disobedience was the kingdom was divided, his son kept two tribes, and the other ten tribes were lost.

From this point forward, I'll only list the rulers of Judah:

3. Rehoboam. Did not do what was right in the sight of the Lord.
4. Abijam. Did not do what was right in the sight of the Lord.
5. Asa. He followed God passionately. Not only did he do what was right in the sight of the Lord in his personal life, but also he aggressively sought out and destroyed idolatry among the people he led. He banished male and female shrine prostitutes, got rid of all the idols, and deposed his grandmother Maacah from her position as queen mother, because she had made an obscene Asherah pole (see 1 Kings 15:11–13). He also removed the foreign altars and the pagan shrines, smashed the sacred pillars, cut down the Asherah poles, and removed the pagan

shrines and incense altars from all of Judah's towns. In essence, Asa called for the people of Judah to repent of their practiced sin. He commanded them to seek the Lord and obey His laws and commands (see 2 Chronicles 14:2–4).

There were benefits from him telling the people to walk away from practiced sin: "So Asa's kingdom enjoyed a period of peace" (2 Chronicles 14:5). During those peaceful years, he was able to build up the fortified towns throughout Judah. No one tried to make war against him during that period. Later a million-man army attacked Asa and Judah, but we read, "They were destroyed by the Lord and His army, and the army of Judah carried off a vast amount of plunder" (1 Chronicles 14:13). Not only was the enemy's army defeated, but Judah got great riches from the attack.

We clearly see the blessing of a leader who not only personally obeyed God and departed from known practiced sin, but called for the people he led to do the same.

6. Jehoshaphat. He also was a king who did what was right in the sight of the Lord both in his personal life and in his leadership. He called for his people to repent of idolatry (known practiced sin). He banished from the land the rest of the male and female shrine prostitutes (see 1 Kings 22:46). He removed the pagan shrines and Asherah poles from Judah (see 2 Chronicles 17:6). In his third year of reigning, he sent officials to teach in all the towns of Judah. They took copies of the law of the Lord and traveled around through all the towns of Judah, teaching the people.

What were the results of Jehoshaphat's leadership? "Then the fear of the Lord fell over all the surrounding kingdoms so that none of them wanted to declare war on Jehoshaphat. Some of the

Philistines brought him gifts. . . . So Jehoshaphat became more and more powerful" (2 Chronicles 17:10–12). Then we read, "Jehoshaphat enjoyed great riches and high esteem" (2 Chronicles 18:1). Armies came against him and Judah, but God caused them to destroy themselves, and Judah received vast amounts of plunder as a result.

We then read, "So the Lord established Jehoshaphat's control over the kingdom of Judah. . . . He became very wealthy and highly esteemed. He was deeply committed to the ways of the Lord" (2 Chronicles 17:5–6).

His big mistake was making an alliance with Ahab's family, who were all idolaters. This almost got him killed, and it ended up corrupting his son. A prophet named Jehu confronted him: "'Why should you help the wicked and love those who hate the Lord?'" (2 Chronicles 19:1–2). However, overall Jehoshaphat and Judah prospered greatly from his obedience, which certainly included confronting the people's practiced sin (idolatry).

7. Jehoram. Did not do what was right in the sight of the Lord.

8. Ahaziah. Did not do what was right in the sight of the Lord.

9. Athaliah (queen). Did not do what was right in the sight of the Lord.

10. Joash. It is recorded of him, "(He) did what was pleasing in the Lord's sight" (2 Chronicles 24:2). However, with regard to his leadership, it's a different story. He didn't tear down the high idolatrous places. In other words, he didn't call for the people he led to repent of their practiced sin. Eventually, we read, "The leaders of Judah . . . persuaded him to listen to their advice. They decided to abandon the Temple of the Lord, . . . and they worshiped Asherah poles and idols instead" (2 Chronicles 24:17–18).

The people he was supposed to influence eventually influenced him; we read that "because of this sin, divine anger fell on Judah and Jerusalem" (verse 18). A prophet came to him and said, "'Why do you disobey the Lord's commands and keep yourselves from prospering?'" (verse 20). Then finally, "In the spring of the year . . . the Aramean army marched against Joash. They . . . killed all the leaders of the nation . . . [took] the plunder back to . . . Damascus. . . . The Arameans attacked with only a small army. The Lord helped them conquer the much larger army of Judah. . . . So judgment was carried out against Joash" (verses 23–24). He was wounded by the Arameans and then assassinated. Joash's reign is an example of a leader not confronting practiced sin and the inevitable terrible consequences.

11. Amaziah. We read, "Amaziah did what was pleasing in the Lord's sight, but not wholeheartedly" (2 Chronicles 25:2). He "did not destroy the pagan shrines, and the people still offered sacrifices and burned incense there" (2 Kings 14:4). The consequences were also not good for the realm. Amaziah defeated Edom and was very proud of it. This led him to challenge Israel's king, Jehoash, to battle. Jehoash warned him to not mess with his nation. Amaziah didn't listen and was "routed" by the army of Israel. He was captured. Then six hundred feet of Judah's wall in Jerusalem was demolished by Israel, and they carried off all the gold and silver and all the articles from the temple of the Lord. Israel seized the treasures from the royal palace, along with the hostages. Amaziah was assassinated (see 2 Chronicles 25:11–28). Again, we see it didn't go well for the leader who started out doing what was pleasing in the Lord's sight, but didn't confront the practiced sin of the people under his leadership.

12. Uzziah. He did what was pleasing in the Lord's sight, and as long as he sought the Lord, God made him prosper. He became very powerful and successful. Although nothing is written about what he did in regard to the idolatrous places of worship, we do know that he personally died a leper because of pride.

13. Jotham. Not much is written about this king. He did what was pleasing in the Lord's sight, but the people continued in their corrupt ways. Sadly, "He did not destroy the pagan shrines, and the people still offered sacrifices and burned incense there" (2 Kings 15:35). The consequences were, "In those days the Lord began to send King Rezin of Aram and King Pekah of Israel to attack Judah" (2 Kings 15:37).

14. Ahaz. Did not do what was right in the sight of the Lord.

15. Hezekiah. Hezekiah's father, Ahaz, was a very wicked king. Ahaz closed the doors to the temple and put a stop to all true worship. The first thing Hezekiah did was to reopen the doors to the temple of the Lord, cleared out all the defiled articles, and repaired the building. It is reported of him, "He did what was pleasing in the Lord's sight, just as his ancestor David had done. He removed the pagan shrines, smashed the sacred pillars, and cut down the Asherah poles. He broke up the bronze serpent that Moses had made, because the people of Israel had been offering sacrifices to it" (2 Kings 18:3–4). He then reinstituted the Lord's Passover festival. It was a huge event and when the people left, they went back to "all the towns of Judah, Benjamin, Ephraim, and Manesseh, and they smashed all the sacred pillars, cut down the Asherah poles, and removed the pagan shrines and altars" (2 Chronicles 31:1).

It is recorded of Hezekiah, "He remained faithful to the Lord in everything, and he carefully obeyed all the commands the

Lord had given Moses. So the Lord was with him, and Hezekiah was successful in everything he did" (2 Kings 18:6–7). The Assyrians came against him, but in the end the angel of the Lord went to the Assyrian camp and killed 185,000 soldiers. Because Hezekiah dealt with the known practiced sin of the people under his leadership, it went very well for both him and the nation.

16. Manasseh. Did not do what was right in the sight of the Lord.

17. Amon. Did not do what was right in the sight of the Lord.

18. Josiah. He was a radically obedient king both in his personal life and leadership. It is recorded of him, "The king read to [all the people of Jerusalem and Judah] the entire Book of the Covenant that had been found in the Lord's Temple" (2 Kings 23:2). He then renewed the covenant, and he instructed the priests to remove all the articles from the Lord's temple that were used to worship Baal, Asherah, and all the powers of heaven. He burned them and placed the ashes on the graves of the people who'd been idolaters.

There is so much to report of what this leader did to get rid of known practiced disobedience. I circled in my Bible every time it states that Josiah "removed, burned, did away with, defiled, destroyed, smashed, cut down, tore down, desecrated, demolished" and any other word used for confronting known sin in Judah. These words occur twenty-five times in just chapter 23 of 2 Kings. It is written of this king, "Never before had there been a king like Josiah, who turned to the Lord with all his heart and soul and strength, obeying all the laws of Moses. And there has never been a king like him since" (2 Kings 23:25). It went well for both him and the people he led during his lifetime.

19. Jehoahaz. Did not do what was right in the sight of the Lord.

20. Jehoiakim. Did not do what was right in the sight of the Lord.

21. Jehoiachin. Did not do what was right in the sight of the Lord.

22. Zedekiah. Did not do what was right in the sight of the Lord.

Let's summarize the story of these kings: In the long run, it went well for the leaders who both lived godly lives and confronted the practiced sin (idolatry) in those they led. This pleasing scenario wasn't true for the nation when the leader led a godly life but avoided confronting the practiced sin of the people.

We should learn from this in the church today. We are heading for difficulty by only giving seekers an invitation to pray a blanket sinner's prayer, void of calling them to true repentance. What if our "new converts" have no plans to turn away from their sins? We then invite idolaters into our community.

We leaders can live godly in our private lives, but if we don't confront the high places of sin among the people, there will be consequences, and the outcome will be similar to the kings listed above. We may have short-term success, but it will not end well. It went well early on for several of the kings who didn't confront the disobedience of their people, but their lack of leadership eventually caught up with them.

If we choose this non-confrontational path of sharing the gospel, we will end up with idolaters who believe they are in right standing with God. In essence, we are exposing our community to spiritual kryptonite.

TAKE ACTION

It's so common to lose the big picture while looking at all the details that we have a saying for it—we lose the forest for the trees. We can do this even while studying God's Word, especially when looking through long periods of history. However, tracking themes throughout a timeline like this chapter does reveal patterns that we otherwise won't see. It shows us the big picture.

The big picture of Israel and Judah's history is that God prospered the leaders when they went beyond getting their own lives right, taking true responsibility for everything God had given them authority over.

You might not be a king or queen. You might not even be a manager or supervisor at work. But you do have a realm over which God has given you authority. The way you take responsibility over that area, and not just your personal life, will have significant influence over how God moves on your behalf. Ask God to reveal your sphere of authority and give you wisdom for how to take responsibility for righteousness in that area. Write down what He tells you, and then make a plan to do it.

ELIMINATING KRYPTONITE

SECTION 4

22

A FACEOFF

Let's start the journey to eliminating kryptonite, both individually and as a community, by first "facing off" with the consequences of neglecting to eradicate this deadly substance.

In junior high school, we were required to take a two-day illegal drug awareness course, which revealed the horrific consequences of drug abuse. In all my wild partying years before I met Christ, I steered clear of any illegal drugs—the fear of the consequences kept me safe.

There certainly is an unhealthy fear, and Jesus has delivered us from it. However, there is a godly fear, similar to what I experienced in school with drugs, which keeps us away from what would take our lives. Scripture states, "Since a promise remains of entering His rest, *let us fear* lest any of you seem to have come short of it" (Hebrews 4:1 NKJV). And "by the fear of the LORD *one* departs from evil" (Proverbs 16:6 NKJV).

Once again, I'll address Christian leaders in this chapter. However, this message should alert all of us, for a believer is "the head and not the tail" (Deuteronomy 28:13). We are all called to be ambassadors of His kingdom, an important position of leadership.

In the light of Scripture, have we thought through our present-day ministry strategy? Why are we hesitant to confront the high places of sin? People with a desire to know God count on us to tell the truth. Yet we omit addressing what keeps them from a genuine relationship. Are we protecting them? Have we considered that we're actually hurting seekers in the long run by avoiding truth? Why deceive those who come to hear about eternal life?

It's no different than Angela, who because of not being told upfront, found herself in a precarious predicament in her marriage. Why would we want anyone to think they can bring practiced sin into a relationship with Jesus? It's impossible. So do we offer a relationship that actually doesn't exist? Is it a counterfeit salvation?

Let's look at this from all angles. We'll consider the outcome of the seekers, the leaders who draw back from addressing kryptonite, and finally the outcome for the church community. The long-run consequences are devastating for all three.

Seekers

We must remember that not a few, not some, but *many* will come to Jesus on the Day of Judgment and fully believe they will be granted entrance into the kingdom of God, but will hear the words, "'Depart from Me, you who practice lawlessness!'" (Matthew 7:23 NKJV).

Who are these people? Are they spiritualists? Are they people of other religions? Are they people caught up in cults? If we examine the words of Jesus, we will discover they are right in our midst; they come to our churches and profess Christianity. He begins by saying, "Not everyone who says to Me, 'Lord, Lord,' shall enter the kingdom of heaven, but he who does the will of My Father in heaven" (Matthew 7:21 NKJV). Jesus identifies people who declare Him Lord. He's not speaking of Joseph Smith, Muhammad, Buddha, Hare Krishna, Confucius, Ra, Sikh, or any other false prophet or god. No, these people—who are denied entrance— call Jesus Christ their "Lord" and say it with passion.

Why is "Lord" duplicated in this verse? Again, as stated earlier, if a word or phrase is repeated twice in Scripture, it is not accidental. The writer is communicating emphasis. However, in cases such as this, it's not just emphasis, but intensity of emotion.

For example, when news reached King David of his son's execution by Joab's army, his highly charged response is, "But the king covered his face, and the king *cried out with a loud voice*, 'O my son Absalom! O Absalom, my son, my son!'" (2 Samuel 19:4 NKJV). Most likely David didn't utter the exact words "my son" twice; rather his outcry of grief was so agonizing that the writer repeated the words so the reader would catch the emphasis of his emotions.

In the same way, the Master is communicating these people's strong sentiments for Him. They are not merely in agreement with the teaching of Jesus Christ being the Son of God; they are emotionally invested and fervent in their belief. We are talking of people who are excited to be Christians, most likely those who are enthusiastic when speaking of their faith.

Not only do they feel deeply for the cause of Christ, but also are involved in His service:

> "I can see it now—at the Final Judgment thousands strutting up
> to Me and saying, 'Master, we preached the Message, we bashed
> the demons, our God-sponsored projects had everyone talking.'"
> (Matthew 7:22 MSG)

The Message paraphrase conveys best that these people weren't sideliners. They were directly involved in or supported the work of their churches. They also are outspoken in their belief of the gospel—"we preached the Message." In essence, they were a part of changing people's lives.

This paraphrased version uses the word "thousands." However, most translations use the word "many." The Greek word is *polus,* defined as "much of number, quantity, amount," and often the word is used in the sense of "mostly." In any case, Jesus is not referring to a small group of people, but a vast group—in fact, quite possibly a majority of the overall number present.

So let's summarize: Jesus is speaking of people who believe in the teachings of the gospel—they call Him Lord, are emotionally invested, give voice to the message, and are active in Christian service. We would easily identify them as true Christians. So what's the separating factor? How do they differ from authentic believers? Jesus tells us, "And then I will declare to them, 'I never knew you; depart from Me, you who practice lawlessness!'" (Matthew 7:23 NKJV).

The obvious key statement is "practice lawlessness." First, what is lawlessness? It is the Greek word *anomia*. *Thayer's Greek Dictionary* defines it as "the condition of [being] without law, because of ignorance of it or because of violating it." Simply put, one who is lawless doesn't adhere to the authority of God's Word. He or she sins on a regular basis without genuine repentance. This person is the modern-day idolater.

Therefore, lawlessness is a form of *kryptonite*.

These men and women don't *periodically* stumble. Rather, they habitually avoid, ignore, neglect, or disobey God's Word. They make a practice of ungodly living—some from believing portions of Scripture don't mean what they say, others from thinking certain Scriptures are not relevant to today, and the majority from believing they are covered by an unscriptural grace.

I sadly believe one of the reasons they continue in sin is because leadership has never confronted them by calling for genuine repentance. They were not told it was impossible to bring their idolatrous lovers into a covenant relationship with Jesus Christ. If truly saved by grace, they'd not only despise the thought, but also choose to walk away from known repetitive sin. They'd crucify their flesh with its passions and desires, and pursue godly character and fruitfulness. This is the mark of a true believer.

It is interesting to note that Jesus declared, "I never knew you." The word "knew" is the Greek word *ginosko*, which means "to intimately know." They've never had a true relationship with Him. Even though they call Him "Master" and "Lord," it's only a title, for they didn't obey Him. The evidence that someone truly has a relationship with God is that they keep His Word:

> Now by this we know that we know Him, if we keep His commandments. He who says, "I know Him," and does not keep His commandments, is a liar, and the truth is not in him.

This statement perfectly lines up with the way Jesus begins this entire discourse: "'You can identify people by their actions'" (Matthew 7:20). The actions Jesus speaks of are not Christian service, speaking the message, or attending church, for those who are turned away from heaven will have these qualities. Today, most would consider a person who calls Jesus "Lord," believes in His teachings, is emotionally involved, and actively participates in Christian service to be a child of God. Yet we've clearly seen from the words of Jesus that these are not the deciding factors in identifying a true believer.

Let me say it like this: You will certainly find these qualities in a true believer. In fact, a person cannot be a true believer without them. However, possessing these qualities doesn't mean someone is a genuine child of God. The deciding question is: Have they repented of known practiced sin and are they passionately seeking to obey Him? A key litmus test is this: *Do they treat His words to "go and sin no more" as optional or mandatory* (see John 5:14)?

The Communicators

Let's now consider the long-term consequences for leaders or communicators of the gospel. The judgment pronounced in Scripture of one who is entrusted with the Word of God and yet withholds communicating the confrontational aspects of truth is sobering. Carefully read this warning God speaks to His messengers:

> "If I *warn* the wicked, saying, 'You are under the penalty of death,' but you fail to deliver the *warning*, they will die in their sins. And I will *hold you responsible* for their deaths. If you *warn* them and they refuse to repent and keep on sinning, they will die in their sins. But you will have *saved yourself* because you obeyed me. If righteous people turn away from their righteous behavior and ignore the obstacles I put in their way, they will die. And if you do not *warn* them, they will die in their sins. None of their righteous acts will be remembered, and I will *hold you responsible* for their deaths. But if you *warn* righteous people not to sin and they listen to you and do not sin, they will live, and you will have *saved yourself*, too." (Ezekiel 3:18–21)

Please observe the frequency of the word "warn" in the above verses. Let me ask an honest question to pastors, leaders, and all believers, for all of us are commissioned to reach the lost and to lovingly confront those who are in sin. Do you want to be held responsible for those you have led to believe they are right with God, yet are not, because you've withheld *warning* them to turn away from practiced sin? They live under the false pretense of being saved, yet due to a lack of *warning* they continue in their sin and will hear on Judgment Day, "Depart from Me."

Could this be why properly preaching the gospel is "*warning* every man and teaching every man in all wisdom, that we may present every man perfect in Christ Jesus" (Colossians 1:28 NKJV). Not only are we to teach, but also to *warn*.

Think about what God made clear in the above verses: "I will hold you

23

┌ TOLERANCE ┐

Let's turn to words spoken directly by our risen King.

In the final book of the Bible, Jesus gives seven messages to seven churches in Asia. If His words were only meant for these historic churches, they would not be found in Scripture. The fact that they are included means they have prophetic application. In other words, they apply to us today, just as they did when they were first spoken.

The Word of God is alive; therefore, we'll look at Jesus's statements as addressing all of us in the present tense. So if the shoe fits, let's wear it—either strengthened by His praise or chastened by His loving correction.

Who Is Jezebel?

The historic church we'll center on is Thyatira. Jesus opens by referring to Himself as the "'Son of God, whose eyes are like flames of fire, whose feet are like polished bronze'" (Revelation 2:18). We could interpret these statements as His eyes are like laser beams that see right to the heart of matters, and His feet are like fine bronze, which describe His almighty strength.

Delightfully, He opens up by praising us, "I know all the things you do. I have seen your love, your faith, your service, and your patient endurance. And I can see your constant improvement in all these things" (Revelation 2:19). It's abundantly clear: He's not addressing a dead church, rather one that is alive and growing.

He begins by acknowledging and complimenting our love. In the death of a church or ministry, it's usually love that wanes and grows cold first, both for God and people. From this tragic state, other fruits of righteousness eventually die off too.

Not surprisingly, this is the focus of the Lord's correction to the very first church at Ephesus—they had left their first love. But not Thyatira. Jesus praises the love of this church. He identifies a community of believers that care for others, and this is very important in the eyes of God. I personally believe this is why Jesus compliments our love before addressing anything else, even before our faith, service, or patience.

The other amazing reality is that this church is *growing* in love, faith, service, and patience. Remarkable! "Maintaining" is not the word that identifies this body of believers; they are consistently advancing in the important areas. *The Message* paraphrase brings this out beautifully: "'I see everything you're doing for Me. Impressive! The love and the faith, the service and persistence. Yes, very impressive! You get better at it every day.'" Any leader or member of a church would be delighted to hear these words spoken by the Lord Himself.

But suddenly His praise turns to correction:

"But I have this complaint against you. You are permitting that woman—that Jezebel who calls herself a prophet—to lead My servants astray. She teaches them to commit sexual sin and to eat food offered to idols. (Revelation 2:20)

There is so much to understand in these words. First of all, let's look at the name *Jezebel*. Is this the actual name of an historic woman? Most commentaries agree it is not. *The New American Commentary: Revelation* states, "There is no occurrence of the name Jezebel in Greco-Roman literature of the time . . . that any Jew would name a daughter Jezebel is no more likely than for Christians to name a child Judas or for Jews to name a child Jesus in eras subsequent to the first century." The *New Living Translation* translators obviously agree with this line of thought for Jesus's words are translated "that Jezebel."

Stating the name like this is similar to when you might refer to someone who is consistently funny as "that comedian." This isn't their name, but rather a depiction of their regular pattern of behavior.

It's safe to say we are dealing with an influential, historic woman who was labeled as a "Jezebel," but that wasn't her actual name. She had a strong influence and eventually a collective group of leaders perpetuated her message. In today's world, it could be one man, woman, or more likely a group of leaders who are propagating the same brand of teaching. Either way, what's important is this philosophy of ministry is affecting the entire church.

Why would the Lord give it this brand? The fruit of it is most likely similar to Jezebel's fruit, the wife of King Ahab of ancient Israel, as found in the books of the Kings. Much could be said about this historic queen, but let's look at her overall impact on Israel. She was a perpetuator of idolatry resulting in the Word of the Lord being silenced in the community, the nation of Israel. Leaders were quieted and the rest of the nation grew slothful to the point of being in a stupor. Only one man, Elijah, had the guts to speak out against this.

Jezebel's influence is evident when Elijah confronts the nation and asks it to choose between obedience to God or practiced sin. This he does in front of the "ministers" who are on her payroll, the prophets of Baal and Asherah. These guys were the media, special interest groups, lawmakers, lawyers, etc., of Elijah's day. The nation had gathered and in the face of these "elites," Elijah challenged the people:

"How long are you going to sit on the fence? If GOD is the real God, follow him; if it's Baal [*practiced sin*], follow him. Make up your minds!" (1 Kings 18:21 MSG)

There is more to following God than silent faith. We are to speak His Word; we are called to be ambassadors. How is this done? Paul makes it clear,

Herald *and* preach the Word! Keep your sense of urgency [stand by, be at hand and ready], whether the opportunity seems to be favorable or unfavorable. [Whether it is convenient or inconvenient, whether it is welcome or unwelcome, you as preacher of the Word are to show people in what way their lives are wrong.] (2 Timothy 4:2 AMPC)

Elijah was the only man in Israel who loved others enough to show the people how their lives were wrong.

Jezebel's impact put fear in the leaders and community. They were now silent, lethargic, intimidated, and would no longer speak out for *Yahweh*. Practiced sin had gained the upper hand, and God's Word was ignored. In the New Testament, a similar effect is beginning to take place in the church. Jesus will not permit it, so He finds a servant, John the apostle—not unlike Elijah—who will speak out.

The Real Issue

Now we must ask, at the church in Thyatira, is Jesus referring to members being physically engaged in sexual immorality and eating food offered to idols? It's possible, but I would lean away from this interpretation, because eating foods offered to idols is not condemned by Paul when writing to two churches (see Romans 14 and 1 Corinthians 10). Why would Jesus identify something as evil that Paul under the inspiration of the Holy Spirit approves? A well-respected commentary states, "Regarding the enticement of the people into sexual immorality, not a few interpreters have suggested that actual sexual promiscuity is unlikely since surely this would have been intolerable in the church. Rather, the reference is to spiritual and/or doctrinal unfaithfulness" (*The New American Commentary: Revelation*).

No matter the case, none of these facts are the focus of Jesus's correction. The action, or rather inaction, being addressed by Jesus is the issue we need to pay attention to, and that is *tolerance*. He says, "'You are *permitting*.'" The Greek word is *eao*. *A Handbook on the Revelation to John* thoroughly defines this word: "The meaning can be expressed positively, 'you allow,' 'you permit,' or negatively, 'you do not forbid,' 'you do not put a stop to,' 'you do not prevent.'"

When you think this through, this is mindboggling. Jesus is past addressing the offender who is, or in our case today, the offenders who are perpetuating a teaching that is seducing His people into idolatry (practiced sin). He clearly states, "I gave her time to repent, but she does not want to turn away" (Revelation 2:21). Obviously, there were previous warnings, but sadly they were unheeded.

Instead He sharply corrects anyone who allows it to continue; in other words, we are not confronting this issue. Instead, we keep teaching only the nice, encouraging, and uplifting parts of the New Testament. In essence we are silent, no different than the people of Israel in the time of Jezebel. It could be compared to this situation: All of us are trapped in a burning building, but none of us does anything to escape or help anyone else escape. We just continue to encourage each other with how blessed we are and keep on expressing our love for each other while the roof and walls are collapsing.

lead many to Jesus, use me to heal sick people, use me to set people free. Father, use me to impact nations for Jesus!" I would pray this over and over, day after day, asking God to launch me in ministry and open doors that no one could shut. I prayed with great passion!

One day that same fall, I was in my normal routine of morning prayer and crying out as I had for many months, even years. All of a sudden in a passionate moment of petitioning, the Holy Spirit spoke to me and said, "Son, you can win multitudes to Jesus, get many free, and heal sick people, and end up in hell forever."

I was baffled. *How could this be? Is this really the Holy Spirit I'm hearing?* I was a little leery of what I'd just heard, until He broke the silence once again by saying, "Son, Judas left his job to follow Me, Judas preached the gospel, he healed the sick in My name, he got people free in My name, and Judas is in hell."

I had been raised Catholic and only been a born-again believer for five years, so what I'm about to describe I was completely unfamiliar with. I trembled, rather quaked, inwardly when I heard His words. I was shaking and afraid to speak. At the same time, I was also completely bewildered, but I knew God was speaking. I was in awe of His presence.

I finally mustered up the strength and reverently asked, "Then what is the thing I should seek for the most? What is first in importance?"

I heard the answer so clearly, "To know Me intimately."

After this encounter, I realized in my personal Bible study that this was the greatest desire of David, Moses, Paul, and all who had finished well in life. Paul states:

Yet indeed I also count all things loss for the excellence of the
knowledge of Christ Jesus my Lord, for whom I have suffered the
loss of all things, and count them as rubbish, that I may gain Christ.
(Philippians 3:8 NKJV)

Similar Dilemmas

The apostle Jude faced a similar dilemma. He wanted to write fellow Christians to encourage them of the wonder of our salvation, but he couldn't. The house was on fire. He had to confront the kryptonite that was creeping into the churches. Look at his words:

> Dear friends, I had been eagerly planning to write to you about the salvation we all share. But now I find that I must write about something else, urging you to defend the faith that God has entrusted once for all time to his holy people. I say this because some ungodly people have wormed their way into your churches, saying that God's marvelous grace allows us to live immoral lives. (Jude 3–4)

This man of God passionately desires to write those he loves about the benefits, blessings, and promises of our life in Christ. He wants to stay in the uplifting and encouraging realm, as most would.

I can relate to his quandary. One of the great emotional battles I often face when writing or teaching is the desire to stay on the "encouragement" side only. I like to be uplifting—who doesn't? However, there is a compelling of the Spirit that pulls us to address that which is seeking to destroy God's precious children.

Therefore, Jude's genuine love compels him to write protective words of warning. What's going on? It's little different than Thyatira. These ungodly perpetrators, who are disguised as pastors, leaders, or believers, either teach or, more likely, model by their lifestyle what he identifies as a "permissive grace," rather than the authentic "empowering grace." In other words, the permissive grace taught doesn't guard us against or enable us to walk away from kryptonite, but permits us to live with little to no godly boundaries. This paves the way for society to dictate our lifestyle due to grace being reduced to merely a covering blanket rather than an enabling force. So, in essence, vulnerable believers are free to follow after the desires of their fallen nature, as modeled by society's culture, thus making them susceptible to kryptonite. This is not the purpose of the grace of God.

Jude is not content with *tolerating* the yeast that is working its way into the churches. He is a true father and is protecting his children from a twisted lifestyle that pulls them away from the life of God. Jesus wouldn't correct him, as He does the leaders of Thyatira; rather, He would commend Jude.

Paul, another caring father, would not stay silent when there were divisions, strife, immorality, lawsuits, covetousness, and other ungodly activities among those in the church. He loved them too much to avoid taking action against the yeast that would spread rapidly throughout the body. James and Peter were no different.

If you read the messages of the early church fathers, they followed suit by using a weapon, the written and proclaimed Word of God, to confront practiced sin among God's people. They spoke out and cast down ideas and justifications formed by culture that were contrary to sound teaching. Jezebel's enforcers didn't intimidate these leaders as they tore down cultural idols!

Silence Gives Consent

When it comes to leadership, silence is nonverbal communication. It communicates agreement and grants permission by saying, "What you're doing is fine." There is an old Latin proverb that states, "Silence gives consent; he ought to have spoken when he was able to." None of the early church fathers or leaders remained silent while kryptonite wormed its way into the lives of those they loved and were responsible for. They spoke out because they saw it as destructive, poisonous, and deadly—able to spread like yeast.

The apostle John states, "The whole world lies under the sway of the wicked one" (1 John 5:19 NKJV). There is a continuous flow of evil in society, the most destructive being *covert evil.* Yes, it's camouflaged with *good.* This deceptive current is identified as "the course of this world" (Ephesians 2:2 NKJV).

Look at it like this: In a river you must paddle against the current to move upstream. We live in a world that has a flow, and these currents are directly opposed to the kingdom of God, but what's more dangerous is they are cunning—masked with *good.* If we don't speak out, this could be compared to lifting our oars and flowing with the current. We may still be pointed upstream, still possessing the appearance and speech of Christianity, but we will be flowing with the social ethics of our day and will lose our effectiveness.

By lifting our oars we avoid dreaded confrontation, yet what we do not confront will not change. Edmund Burke wrote, "All that is necessary for evil to triumph is that good men do nothing." The cultural idols in the hearts and minds of believers develop a stronger hold when leaders remain silent.

As the deception increases, what we tolerate eventually sedates us. We now empathize and even align with what saps our supernatural strength. We no longer are a counterculture, but a subculture. We have the label of "Christianity," but are not *ambassadors of power* but rather *agents of confusion.* The world around us questions, "We see your churches, hear your music and the teaching of love and grace, but where is the evidence of your Almighty God?"

Paul boldly declares those who profess Christianity but align with the flow of the world are actually enemies of the cross. Yes, enemies!

> For I have told you often before, and I say it again with tears in my eyes, that there are many whose conduct shows they are really enemies of the cross of Christ. They are headed for destruction.

Their god is their appetite, they brag about shameful things, and they think only about this life here on earth. But we are citizens of heaven, where the Lord Jesus Christ lives. (Philippians 3:18–20)

Read the first verse carefully; first there is "many." Second, it's not their words that show they are enemies, for they verbally acknowledge Jesus. "Such people claim they know God, but they deny him by the way they live" (Titus 1:16). They're camouflaged with godly appearances, but show they are enemies by behavior; driven by the appetites of the flesh—lust, pleasure, status, popularity, sexual vices, gossip, and more.

Paul speaks out—he confronts and doesn't tolerate. Read his letters and see just how often he warns and corrects us of ungodly and worldly behavior. But remember this is actually God's Word coming through Paul's pen to us.

Direct confrontation by proclaiming what God's Word states is the only way to tear down these strongholds. If we don't directly oppose them with Scripture, we allow these philosophical fortresses to continue to gain strength in the hearts and minds of believers, as well as those who are lost. Our refusal to speak out opens the door to kryptonite's influence.

Contrasting Results

What are Jesus's concluding words to our church? They are not for the faint of heart. He clearly states that those who buy into false teaching will "suffer greatly" unless they repent. This will be a sign, and all churches will know that He searches our thoughts and intentions and will give to each of us whatever we deserve (see Revelation 2:22–23).

But here is the great news: He says to those who do not buy into kryptonite—those who hold on tightly to His Spirit and His Word—they will be given authority over the nations . . . the same authority given to Jesus by our Father.

The results are quite contrasting: one is foreboding consequences and the other is unfathomable rewards. Can we afford not to pay careful attention to these instructions, especially since they are straight from the mouth of our resurrected King?

TAKE ACTION

Jezebel pressured God's prophets into silence, and even killed many of them. Only one was willing to speak up on the Lord's behalf, yet look at what God was willing to do for that one. He protected him, provided for him, and supported him with supernatural signs and wonders that still make us marvel today.

God is still looking for those who will stand and speak for truth. This isn't just trying to be critical. We're not sin-hunters. But at the same time, we cannot allow ourselves to be intimidated into silence, worrying that people will see us as backward, intolerant, or some other label.

The first step is to heed this warning in your own life. Whatever it takes, get free from the sins you have given yourself to in the past. Once you are free, get to work freeing others, diligently warning them of the dangers of sin; Paul writes "being ready to punish all disobedience when your obedience is fulfilled" (2 Corinthians 10:6 NKJV).

If you don't like confrontation, ask God to give you a love for others that will compel you to confront them. Make this your next target to overcome. Then, by God's grace, you can help others overcome it too.

24

LOVE AND TRUTH

Now we come to the most critical aspect of eliminating kryptonite—the motive behind killing it. The lack or absence of this mighty force to destroy kryptonite is most likely the motivation behind the pendulum swing in our way of presenting the gospel and philosophy of ministry. The force I'm speaking of is nothing other than *the love of God*. Paul makes a powerful statement to us:

> We will not be influenced when people try to trick us with lies so clever they sound like the truth. Instead, we will *speak the truth in love*, growing in every way more and more like Christ. (Ephesians 4:14–15)

False teachings, similar to what Jesus addresses in Thyatira, as well as what is described in the letters of Jude, Peter, John, and Paul, are all so clever they can be easily mistaken for the truth. The enemy is much smarter than we give him credit for. If he could mislead Eve in a perfect environment, permeated with the presence of God, how much easier is it for him to deceive in our corrupted environment? And what might protect us from the deception of false teachings?

The answer is the truth, but not truth alone—truth *spoken in love*. Truth apart from love directs us down the road of the "letter of the law," that which kills: *legalism*. This ultimately helps fuel and support deception and is the cause of the avoidance or even elimination of scriptural warnings, which are so crucial to the health of the church.

We get beat up by legalism, because it's nasty, cruel, and hateful. To counteract its brutality, we emphasize love. But love spoken without the truth is not love at all. It's a counterfeit. It's a form of kindness, sympathy, tenderness, and patience, all having the appearance of being godly love. But if these virtues are outside of truth, we will also inevitably wind up on the road of deception.

Let's be candid; we steer clear from speaking certain scriptural truths because we view them as being outside of the love we so earnestly desire. The truths we avoid call for people not to stay as they are, but to make lifestyle changes. We view calling men and women to repentance as a lack of compassion, tenderness, kindness, and love. Yet consider this: I see a blind man heading straight for a cliff that will cause him to fall to certain death. I could let the disaster occur because my intervention might be perceived as negative or intolerant of the man's choice of direction. If I don't get him to stop and make a course correction, he will die. If I positively encourage him by making uplifting comments but don't call for a course adjustment, then I will make his final steps more enjoyable, but he'll still end up at the bottom of the canyon, dead. Is any of this true love?

In our society, and with many in the church, such genuine love is perceived as bigoted and hateful. This stronghold has emerged with many believers as a result of viewing life through the perspective of seventy or eighty years rather than through the lens of eternity. Consider this example: If my perspective of happiness is one day in length, I can attend a wedding reception that has a table full of desserts and eat every one of them. I will have an enjoyable, happy day. However, if I have a six-month perspective on happiness, I will treat the table differently. I will only eat one

and has many other similarities to the love of God. However, the definition that ultimately distinguishes the love of God from the world's love is found in these words: "This is the love of God, that we keep His commandments" (1 John 5:3 NKJV).

In case we missed this vital definition in his first letter, John, known as the apostle of love, gives it again in his second letter:

"This is love, that we walk according to His commandments." (2 John 6 NKJV)

This is different than the apostle Paul's "love is" as found in 1 Corinthians. John doesn't give the descriptive aspects of love, but offers the very core definition—what distinguishes God's love from all other forms. Love is keeping Jesus's commandments. The Lord makes this clear at the Last Supper:

"Those who accept My commandments and obey them are the ones who love Me." (John 14:21)

So if I'm kind, patient, tender, not jealous, not rude, not boastful, and not irritable—but am cheating regularly on my wife or my taxes—I'm not walking in the love of God.

If I'm kind, patient, tender, not jealous, not rude, not boastful, and not irritable, but I approve and condone sexual immorality, such as homosexuality, which is now increasingly approved and encouraged even by the government in many nations, then I'm not walking in the love of God.

In fact, I'm deceived and in a more dangerous place than the man who is rude, jealous, boastful, and irritable, because he probably knows he is away from God. I, in error, may think I am in good standing with God, because someone led me in a "sinner's prayer," but I never repented of my practiced sin. Simply put, I am not heeding Jesus's commandments.

At this point, allow me to inject this very important point: I do not keep God's commands to be saved. Rather, I walk in them because I am saved and have His love abiding in me. Being obedient is the evidence that I have truly surrendered my heart and life to Him.

Again, the truth is, any form of love that directly contradicts God's Word and ways is not the love that endures forever. It is temporary. It will cause people to feel good, even sacrificial, and will provide inclusion and acceptance, but it will not be eternal. It does not lead to everlasting life. It will one day fall off a cliff into the eternal pit of the lake of fire.

Why, then, is this love, which seems so right, temporary? Adam and Eve judged the fruit of the tree of the knowledge of good and evil to be good and that it would make them wise.

> When the woman saw that the tree was *good* . . . a tree desirable
> to make one *wise*. (Genesis 3:6 NKJV)

Eve's initial thoughts most likely went down the path of, *Why would a loving God ever tell us not to eat what is "good" for us? This doesn't make any logical sense.* She chose to embrace the "good" and "wisdom" that is outside of God's counsel. We want to know the "why," but let's be straightforward: There are some things God wants us to obey even when we don't understand the why behind them. Can we believe He loves us when He tells us to stay clear of what seems good for us? Can His character be trusted? Or do we become the judges who tell Him what is good for us, no different than the couple did in the Garden of Eden?

There are so many examples that could be given of God's mysteries or the why behind God's directives, but let me give just one. After almost forty years, I haven't met a person who can give me the why behind God telling a prophet, "'You must not eat or drink anything while you are there, and do not return to Judah by the same way you came'" (1 Kings 13:9). The prophet didn't obey this *seemingly senseless* command, but in the end lost his life because of disobedience.

To be candid, true love can sometimes seem contrary to what feels like love. Why would Paul say to the Corinthian church, "I will gladly spend myself and all I have for you, even though it seems that the more I love you, the less you love me" (2 Corinthians 12:15)? It makes little sense that this community of believers would see Paul as not being loving! I believe the obvious answer is they viewed him as a dogmatic, legalistic leader, one who wanted to keep them under the rules, so to speak. Perhaps their opinion of him went to the level of seeing him as a bigot. But that wasn't the truth at all. He loved them with the *everlasting love*, not the world's version of love. He confronted them with truth, warned them, and called them to repentance, which may have seemed unloving to his hearers. But his words were saturated with the true love of God.

Speaking the Truth in Love

With all this said, now let's turn to discussing the importance of true love. Let's review love's descriptions:

Love is patient.
Love is kind.
Love is not jealous.
Love is not boastful.
Love is not proud.
Love is not rude.
Love does not demand its own way.
Love is not irritable.
Love keeps no record of being wronged.
Love does not rejoice about injustice.
Love never gives up.
This is love, to keep His commandments.

If we speak the truth and are not kind, not patient, but rather jealous, boastful, proud, rude, demand our own way, irritable, keep records of how we've been wronged, unforgiving, rejoice at injustice, and give up on people, we are not keeping His commandments. So we can preach repentance, faith in Jesus Christ, and all that is found in Scripture, but we are not operating in true love. We have entered into the realm of legalism and will hurt people, rather than bring them to God.

I had a young man approach me one day and say, "I'm called to the ministry you operate in. I'm called to bring correction to the body of Christ!"

I knew in my heart his motive was off when he said this to me. The Holy Spirit gave me these words for him: "Do you want to know how to operate in true prophetic ministry?"

His face lit up and he immediately said, "Yes, I would love to know."

"The entire time you are bringing any form of correction or warnings, your heart burns in love for the people you are speaking to," I said.

He was speechless for a few moments. "Wow, God has some work He needs to do with me."

I said to him, "I'm so proud of you. It takes a humble man to say this. You are closer to being at that place than you even know. Your heart is tender."

Love cares more for the other person than for yourself. It cares enough to not permit anyone to walk off a cliff. It will exude all the tender characteristics as described in 1 Corinthians 13, but in doing so it will never deviate from the commandments of our Savior and God.

Love is so vital, so important, it's the essence of life. Pray that God fills your heart with His love, with Himself, so that you would truly care more for others than your own life. We are told that the Holy Spirit pours out this love in our hearts. We can ask for it—the depth, length, and height of His life-giving love.

So ask, ask again, then keep on asking Him to fill your heart with divine, eternal love.

We must speak up against the sin that seeks to invade the church, but we must do it in love or our warnings will not have the intended result. God warns us continually throughout the Bible, yet His earnest love called Him to do even more—sending His Son to pay the price for all the sins He warned us not to do.

This is the love we must have as we warn people against sin. And there is only one source of love—God. God is love. If we want to grow in love, we must grow in our fellowship with God.

It is vital beyond words for us to spend regular time with God, asking and seeking Him to fill us with more of His love. When we are filled with love, it will drive out our fears of confrontation. It will compel us to take action on behalf of those around us, not just through humanitarian causes, but to warn when needed. God's love will set us free and enable us to bring that freedom to others. Set aside time today to pray earnestly—don't give up quickly—that God would fill you with His love.

25

KILLING
KRYPTONITE

Three scenarios plague believers when it comes to sin.

First, there are those who choose to overlook sin because of their hardened hearts. They are immune to the reality of breaking God's heart. The Lord laments over them, "'Are they ashamed of these disgusting actions? Not at all—they don't even know how to blush!'" (Jeremiah 8:12). Their conscience is compromised, sometimes even to the point of being seared.

Second, and just as dangerous, are those who buy into the lie that we are all sinners by nature and the blood of Jesus is powerful enough to free us from the penalty, but not the bondage of sin. These firmly hold to the truth that in Christ we are made holy, but believe the lie that it's unnecessary to live a sanctified life. This was the brand of teaching being propagated in the church of Thyatira. Paul specifically addresses this mindset when writing:

> Well then, should we keep on sinning so that God can show us
> more and more of His wonderful grace? Of course not! Since we
> have died to sin, how can we continue to live in it? (Romans 6:1–2)

These first two scenarios are clearly identified as kryptonite, which is known, practiced sin that weakens a believer, as well as any community of believers. Those who fall in these two categories are *given to sin*. They are the ones who will hear Jesus say, "Depart from Me," on Judgment Day (see Matthew 7:20–23).

Third are those who are in a struggle to break free from sin. They want out, but it has a tight grip on them. They haven't yet discovered from God's Word how to exercise their freedom by faith. When they sin, their hearts are broken because of their love for God. They truly repent, but in time fall into sin again. Sadly, one of the things that keeps them in bondage is the guilt and condemnation of what they're bound to. The shame of their sin holds them down.

If you are in this third group, please hear me. Jesus tells us, "'If another believer sins, rebuke that person; then if there is repentance, forgive. Even if that person wrongs you seven times a day and each time turns again and asks forgiveness, you must forgive'" (Luke 17:3–4). The reason our Master tells us to forgive someone who sins, yet genuinely repents multiple times per day, is because we are to forgive as our Heavenly Father forgives us (see Ephesians 4:32). Please know, if you have sinned multiple times but each time genuinely approach God, broken-hearted in true repentance, you are forgiven and the blood of Jesus cleanses you as if you've never sinned. Don't punish yourself, as this takes away from the greatness of the blood of Jesus and puts righteousness back on your own works. You can never be saved or forgiven by doing this. Forgiveness is God's gracious gift.

It is this third scenario I would like to address in this chapter. I want to share my story of how God's Word set me free.

I Couldn't Get Free

When I was twelve years old, some friends introduced me to pornographic magazines. We would share them with each other and needless to say, it wasn't long before I became addicted.

It started out with milder porn but quickly advanced to the hard-core material. This led to sexual fantasies that were uncontrollable in my mind. I would sit in my high school classes, stare at girls, and envision us having sexual encounters. I was consumed with sexual lust.

At the age of nineteen, I gave my life to Jesus Christ at a meeting in my fraternity house. Many sins immediately lost their power over my life: drunkenness, cussing, inappropriate behavior with girls, crudeness, and many other ungodly behaviors just seemed to fade away. However, pornography and lust didn't lose their hold. I was still bound and not able to walk away. Every time I succumbed to this sin, I quickly repented and sincerely asked God for forgiveness.

Prior to being saved, I didn't give a second thought to my driving sexual lust, but just yielded anytime the desire arose. After being saved, I was now in a vicious battle. I didn't want to look at porn because I knew it was contrary to godly behavior, but it seemed to be more powerful than my strength to resist.

In 1982, at the age of twenty-three, I married Lisa. I thought the lust would fade away because now I was married to the girl of my dreams. But it didn't and actually grew worse. If there was pornography anywhere in my vicinity I would gravitate toward it—almost like steel shavings are attracted to a magnet. It affected Lisa's and my relationship, both in bed and in other areas of intimacy.

In 1983, I entered the ministry and still battled with porn. My conviction that it was wrong was growing stronger. My position of serving in church was to take care of our pastor, his family, and any of our guest ministers. Our church was one of the most recognized churches in America, and we hosted many notable visiting pastors and speakers. One of them was well-known for his deliverance ministry. He'd been in Asia for several years, and the documented stories of how people got free from vices or demons were phenomenal, sometimes even mind-blowing. God used him in a most profound way. His name was Lester Sumrall.

In the fall of 1984, he came to our church to do a four-day seminar, and I was once again his host. I'd gotten to know him quite well from his previous visits. This time when I was transporting him in the vehicle and we were alone, it seemed like an opportune time for me to open up and share my struggle with sexual lust. I humbled myself and was brutally honest because I wanted out! Lester spoke sternly as a true father in the faith would. I listened carefully to every word, then desperately asked him, "Please pray for my freedom."

He prayed a very strong prayer, but to my disappointment, in the weeks and months that followed, I experienced no change. I continued to fight lust afterward.

Approximately nine months later, I was offered the use of a condominium to get away to fast and pray. On the fourth day of the fast, I'll never forget the date—it was May 6, 1985—I was completely delivered from that spirit of lust while deep in prayer. The Holy Spirit led me to fervently command lust to leave my life. I did, and the authority that came on me was beyond anything I'd ever experienced. I'm still free today, thank God!

Why Later?

After walking in freedom for a couple of years, a nagging question arose, which I took to the Lord in prayer. "Father," I asked, "I don't understand. I humbled myself before Lester, this great man of God. Since many have been delivered through his ministry, why wasn't I set free that day he prayed for me? Why was it nine months before I became free?"

The Lord started showing me my life in that time period. During the fall of 1984, when Lester came to speak, I was praying every morning for at least ninety minutes. I'd been doing this for a couple of years. I would get up at 5:00 a.m. and was outside by myself by 5:30 a.m. and prayed until 7:00 a.m. My most passionate prayers at the time were, "God use me to

His pursuit was to know Jesus intimately and out of that knowledge would exude powerful ministry. I'd been chasing after ministry, rather than to know Jesus intimately. That day everything changed.

Now my primary focused prayers every morning went something like this, "Lord, I want to know You the best a man can know You. I want to please You the best a man can please You. Show me Your heart, reveal to me what is important to You, and show me what is not so important to You. Teach me Your ways and may my life bring joy to You . . ."

I would still go out early in the morning, but my passionate pleas were now along this line. I didn't realize what was happening, but God later would show me.

So the answer to my question of, "Why didn't I get free when Lester Sumrall prayed for me?" was coming into focus. God then spoke to me and said, "When you opened up to the evangelist, you were afraid the sin of lust would keep you from the ministry you knew I'd called you to. You were fearful it would disqualify you. The focus of your sorrow was you; it was a worldly sorrow."

He continued, "Nine months later, because you had been crying out to know Me intimately, your heart was breaking because you were hurting My heart by your sin. You knew I had died to free you from this sin, and you hated participating in anything that was along the lines of what sent Me to the cross. The focus of your sorrow was on Me; it was a godly sorrow."

Paul states to the Corinthian church,

Now I rejoice, not that you were made sorry, but that your sorrow led to repentance. For you were made sorry in a godly manner, that you might suffer loss from us in nothing. For *godly sorrow* produces repentance leading to salvation, not to be regretted; but the *sorrow of the world* produces death. (2 Corinthians 7:9–10 NKJV)

The Greek word for "salvation" in this verse doesn't necessarily mean to be born again. It is the word, *soteria*, which is defined as, "safety, deliverance, preservation from danger or destruction" (WSNTDICT). Let's isolate the word "deliverance" in this definition and insert it in the above verse: "For godly sorrow produces repentance leading to *deliverance*." I was delivered—set free, and it was godly sorrow that opened the door to secure it.

Two Sorrows

Two kinds of sorrows—one is godly, one is worldly. How are each distinguished? King Saul's and King David's experiences illustrate the difference. As discussed in a previous chapter, Saul disobeys God in the incident of the Amalekites. When he is called out by the prophet Samuel he denies it, but Samuel doesn't relent. Then Saul puts the blame on the people; only after the prophet's persistence does Saul finally say, "I have sinned." Once he's confessed, he then quickly says to Samuel, "'I have sinned; yet honor me now, please, before the elders of my people and before Israel'" (1 Samuel 15:30 NKJV). The focus of Saul's sorrow is himself. Samuel had embarrassed him by confronting him in front of his leadership team and the people. He wants his honor restored.

King David, on the other hand, greatly sins. He commits adultery with another man's wife, and manipulates the murder of her husband to cover his sin. The prophet Nathan confronts him in front of his leadership team and people. The moment the sin is exposed, David falls to the ground and says, "I have sinned against the Lord" (2 Samuel 12:13 NKJV).

Saul said, "I've sinned." David said, "I've sinned *against the Lord*." There's the difference. David is heartbroken that he has hurt the heart of the One he loves. His sorrow is not focused on himself, as Saul's was. This is confirmed when David lies before the Lord all night and fasts seven days. He's utterly sorry for what he's done against God. He makes this abundantly clear when he cries out:

> Against You, You only, have I sinned, and done this evil in Your sight—that You may be found just when You speak, and blameless when You judge. (Psalm 51:4 NKJV)

Sorrow of the world focuses on us—What are the consequences? Will I be judged? Will I be disqualified? Will I suffer from my sin? What will people think of me?—and so forth. Godly sorrow focuses on Jesus; I've hurt the heart of the One I love, and no matter what He decides: *His justice is fair and true and I fall before His mercy.*

Walk It Out

I was now free, but I still needed my mind to be renewed. This took two or three years. Before May of 1985, if pornography was anywhere in my vicinity, I couldn't resist its draw. Now I was able to resist and had the ability to turn away. But if a nice-looking woman walked by me in tight clothing, I would have to turn my eyes the other way to not give opportunity for my thoughts to go awry. This is not the full freedom Jesus provides for us. The deliverance wasn't yet complete.

There is a difference between *being set free* and *being made free*. I was set free on May 6, but Jesus says, "And you shall know the truth, and the truth shall *make* you free" (John 8:32 NKJV). The goal is to be *made* free, and it takes truth permeating our being to do this.

As time went by, I stayed in His Word and prayer, and my mind started seeing things the way He sees them in regard to women. The first paradigm shift occurred when the realization flooded my heart that all women are *daughters*. I know that doesn't sound like a deep thought, but it truly was for me. The Holy Spirit showed me that every woman is some mommy and daddy's little girl. They are not a piece of meat, as I'd seen them before my deliverance.

A while later, an even greater revelation came into my heart. It became clear to me that all women are created in God's image, and He has crowned them with glory and honor (see Genesis 1:26–27 and Psalm 8:5). Again, this may not sound profound, but it was a life-changing revelation in the core of my being.

Now, if pornography is flashed before me, it is offensive! Yes, what I was once enamored by, now actually repulses me. Now, if an attractive woman walks past me I don't have to turn my head as I did for a few years after being set free. I can now look her in the eye and warmly say, "Hello," without any inappropriate desire for her.

I discovered the power of the grace of Jesus Christ. I realize most Christians see grace as salvation, forgiveness of sins, and an unmerited gift. But that is where it ends for the majority. I came to realize that God's grace is all these amazing attributes, but it also empowers us to change, to do what truth calls us to do.

Can we possibly believe that Jesus's free gift delivers us from the eternal *penalty of sin*, but is not powerful enough to free us from the *bondage of sin?* You can never convince me otherwise.

I know! I've experienced His life-transforming grace and now am free. I'm so thankful that He did this for me, and I'm so thankful He'll do the same for you! It was a battle, not a walk in the park; it took persistence and fervent prayer. Most likely, it will be the same for you. The good news is you cannot fail because God's grace and love cannot fail. So stay with it and be made free.

TAKE ACTION

God is your Savior, and there is no other. No five-step program, no human effort, and no list of rules can set you free from the bondage of sin. But that doesn't mean God delivers us from our sin while we do nothing. God will deliver you, but pursuing Him requires action. Pursuing our Heavenly Father with the right motives—to know Him, not to get something from Him—is what will lead to your deliverance.

The question is, how important is it to you to get free? Will you make time to seek God? Will you take retreats away if you need to? Will you cry out and not stop until you've found His presence and laid hold of His promises? Will you approach Him, allowing Him to set the agenda for your relationship? Will you pursue freedom from sin for the sake of your relationship and not just because it hinders the life you want? Will you humble yourself to let established, godly leaders pray for you and speak into your life?

Count the cost of your bondage, but also count the cost of your freedom. Then go after God with your whole heart. He is waiting to know you intimately!

26

THE SIN THAT'S NOT SIN

Did you raise an eyebrow when you read this chapter title?

There is another aspect of idolatry that we've not yet covered, and it can be identified as *the sin that's not sin*. To complete the process of eliminating kryptonite, we can't ignore this one, for it can be the most elusive to identify. Let's open with a parable.

One day a bystander commented to Jesus about how great it will be to attend a banquet in the kingdom of God. Jesus takes advantage of his comment to illustrate a profound truth. He says, "'A man prepared a great feast and sent out many invitations. When the banquet was ready, he sent his servant to tell the guests, 'Come, the banquet is ready.' But they all began making *excuses*'" (Luke 14:16–18). The pivotal word in this parable is "excuses."

Have you ever experienced this? You ask something of someone, whether it's for help, an invitation to a party or dinner, to accomplish a needed task or to run an errand, or any other request, and the reply is a lame excuse. What do excuses communicate? Quite simply that what they want to do is more important than your request. In essence, they are saying, "My priorities are higher on my list than yours."

According to Jesus, this man wasn't throwing a barbeque, serving hamburgers and hot dogs with some chips. This was a great feast, an important event. He did it to bless those he would invite. The invitations had been printed, sealed, and sent out to everyone he desired to attend, but everyone replied with excuses: "One said, 'I have just bought a field and must inspect it. Please excuse me'" (Luke 14:18).

Here is the important question: Is it a sin to purchase a field? Of course not. If it is, I'm in trouble because I've bought some land in my lifetime. However, when purchasing the land is more important than the Word of the Lord, it is sin—"sin that's not sin." More specifically, it's idolatry or kryptonite.

Let's look at the next man: "Another said, 'I have just bought five pairs of oxen, and I want to try them out. Please excuse me'" (Luke 14:19).

Again, is buying oxen, or to be more relevant, is buying equipment for your business a sin? Of course it isn't—I've bought business equipment in my lifetime. However, when buying something is more important than the Word of the Lord, it is sin. So again, it's sin that's not sin, or more specifically, it's idolatry or kryptonite.

Let's check out the last recipient of the invitation:

"Another said, 'I now have a wife, so I can't come.'" (Luke 14:20)

One last time, allow me to ask, is marrying a wife a sin? If it is, a lot of men, including me, are in trouble. Of course it isn't. However, when the wife becomes more important than the Word of the Lord, it is sin. Again, it's sin that's not sin, or more specifically, it's idolatry or kryptonite.

I think the point is clear: when we put anyone, anything, or any activity before the Word of the Lord, what is not sin becomes sin.

My Kryptonite Exposed

As I've mentioned before, I fell in love with Jesus Christ when I was a sophomore at Purdue University. I received Him as Lord at my fraternity in 1981. I was on fire for Him!

Several months later, it was the football season at Purdue. I was now a junior, and as a student, I had season tickets to all our home games. During the previous two years, I didn't miss one of them. But now, I was so excited about Jesus, I used the time of the football games to study my Bible. The fraternity was quiet because all the guys were at the game. It was a chance for some great times of prayer. I was enjoying time with God more than football games.

No one had said to me, "You shouldn't go to the football games." I never thought attending a game was wrong. In fact, I went to many of them my final year.

Just after graduating from Purdue, I moved to Dallas, Texas, and several months later accepted the position at my church. Due to the size and influence of the ministry, we had over four hundred employees.

At that time, the Dallas Cowboys were one of the best teams in the National Football League. I wasn't much of a Cowboys fan since I had grown up in Michigan, but I frequently heard guys on staff talking about the team every Monday. They would passionately discuss in detail the previous day's game—stats, notable plays and, of course, the potential playoff picture.

Out of curiosity, I started watching the Cowboys. It started out with a quarter or two. I liked watching them because they were exciting. There was another benefit; it gave me the opportunity to intelligently discuss the games with the guys at the office.

But as time passed, my interest in the Cowboys became stronger, and I started watching entire games. I found myself talking to the TV with great passion, cheering and sometimes yelling at the players. It eventually got to the place that I didn't miss a game or any portion of one. Even in the offseason, my coworkers and I continued conversations about the draft and how great the Cowboys would be the next season. I was now a full-blown fan!

Once the next season arrived, I was consumed with excitement. Every

Sunday after service I would rush home, flip on the TV, and not even remove my church clothes—and we wore suits in those days. Sometimes I would just sit there glued to the television, even though I was in uncomfortable clothes and needed to use the bathroom. I didn't want to miss a play.

At halftime, I would change clothes. If Lisa needed help with something, forget it. "Honey, the Cowboys are playing," I'd say. We'd eat at halftime or even better, after the game—but never during the game.

At this point, I knew all the stats of the team. I'd carefully examine them and constantly think about how the Cowboys could do better. I was the one leading the conversations at work. There were some people at my church who had season tickets, and I'd accept every invitation they made to go to the stadium for a game. There was never a *lame excuse* to not go.

Let's fast-forward to the next season. A short time earlier, I had prayed something I thought to be quite simple and seemingly insignificant. However, I didn't realize it would change my life. My prayer was, "Lord, I ask that you would purify my heart; I want to be holy, set apart for You, so if there's anything in my life not pleasing to You or a priority before You, expose it and help me remove it."

The football season was coming to a close and the playoffs were approaching. It was the day of a crucial game. The Cowboys were playing the Philadelphia Eagles, and the winner of the game would go to the playoffs and the loser was out. I was glued to the television—not seated on a couch, but standing on my feet right in front of the screen. The game was in the final quarter with only eight minutes left on the clock. The Cowboys were behind by four points, but their star quarterback had the team moving down the field. I was now pacing the floor between plays, yelling in frustration at miscues or reacting with exuberant joy over great plays. The suspense was exhilarating.

All of a sudden, without any advance notice, the Spirit of God prompted me to pray. A sudden urge overwhelmed me—*pray, pray, pray!* It was a burden, a strong and weighty feeling deep in my heart. I had come to recognize this urging when the Spirit of God desires you to pull away and pray.

I said out loud, "Lord, there are only eight minutes left in this game. I'll pray when it's over."

The urge continued, and it was not letting up.

A few minutes went by. Still looking for relief, I exclaimed, "Lord, I'll pray five hours when this game is over. There's only six more minutes left!"

The Cowboys were moving the ball down the field. I just knew they would come back and win this important game. However, the urge to pray still didn't lift off me. In fact, it was stronger. I was frustrated. I didn't want to pull away from the game.

I then said aloud, "Lord, I'll pray the rest of the day, even through the night if that is what You desire!"

I watched the rest of the game. The Cowboys won, and since I had made a promise to God, I immediately turned off the television. I went straight up the stairs to my office, closed the door, and got down on the carpet floor to pray. But the urge to pray was no longer present. There was no longer a burden of any sort, not even a slight feeling. There was nothing.

I tried to work it up. I tried to pray and my words were stale and flat. It didn't take long to realize what had happened. I chose the game over God's request. I had a *lame excuse* that took precedence over His request.

I dropped my face into the carpet and moaned, "God, if anyone asked me, 'Who is more important to me, God or the Dallas Cowboys?' I would without hesitation respond, 'God, of course!' But I just showed who was more important. You needed me, but I chose the football game over You. Please forgive me!"

I heard immediately in my heart, "Son, I don't want your sacrifice of five hours of prayer; I desire obedience."

Any Area of Life

This type of idolatry can happen in any area of life. I recall, in the same time period, a morning when I was getting ready to pour my cereal in a bowl. I love my cereal in the morning! But that morning, I heard God whisper, "I want you to fast breakfast."

I recall looking at that cereal and wanting it so bad. I said, "Lord, I'll go on a three-day fast next week,"—another *lame excuse* to not obey what He'd asked of me. He showed me from this how food was an idol in my life. I'd missed precious opportunities with Him, because my desire for food outweighed my desire to experience His presence and Word.

In a similar fashion, when later my love for golf got out of place, the Holy Spirit prompted me one day to give my entire set of clubs to another pastor (it wasn't out of place in his life).

After a year and a half of not playing, the Lord put it on the heart of a professional golfer to give me thousands of dollars' worth of his golf equipment. I was puzzled. Then, a few months later, a pastor told me God had put it in his heart to give me his set of golf clubs. Now I was really confused!

Later when alone, I asked the Lord, "What do I do with all this golf equipment?"

"Go play golf," I heard in my heart.

"But You had me walk away from the sport and give all my clubs away a year and a half ago."

"Golf is no longer out of place for you," I heard God say. "It's now recreation and enjoyment for you."

I've played the game ever since, and God has used it in a wonderful way to bring rest and refreshment. It's also become an avenue to get people saved who were lost, and for me to connect with my sons, church leaders, and ministry partners. In fact, over five million dollars for mission outreaches have been donated to Messenger International through golfing with friends and partners at our Messenger Cup golf tournaments. If I had totally cut golf off for the rest of my life, this wouldn't have happened. Golf was no longer kryptonite.

These were areas of sin that aren't sin. We can do this with business, ministry, sports, relationships, pleasurable things, even essential things in life. The list is as endless as there are things, activities, relationships, and positions.

God desires for us to enjoy this life. In fact, I find an amazing comment by the apostle Paul:

> God, Who richly and ceaselessly provides us with everything for [our] enjoyment. (1 Timothy 6:17 AMPC)

He wants us to experience all the wonderful blessings He's given us. He wants us to enjoy life. He only asks to remain first on our priority list, which means He and His desires get precedence any time, any place, and during any activity.

No lame, or even good, excuses!

Don't Miss the Banquet!

Let's turn to the conclusion of Jesus's parable. We've read of the three who were invited to the feast but made excuses. Now we read:

> "The servant returned and told his master what they had said. His master was furious and said, 'Go quickly into the streets and alleys of the town and invite the poor, the crippled, the blind, and the lame.' After the servant had done this, he reported, 'There is still room for more.' So his master said, 'Go out into the country lanes

and behind the hedges and urge anyone you find to come, so that the house will be full. For none of those I first invited will get even the smallest taste of my banquet.'" (Luke 14:21–24)

This certainly refers to the marriage supper of the Lamb, the feast God the Father will throw for His Son in the end. We are all invited. However, there is a principle here that applies to the here and now. When God invites us to something that interrupts our daily routine or the things we like so much, it means there is something much greater He has in store for us. It's called a divine encounter that will end up being a banquet, a feast of His Word, wisdom, presence, provision, counsel, power, or any of many other wonderful blessings only He can give.

He had something in store for me during that Dallas Cowboys game. One day I will find out what it was—I'm sure He found someone in a "country lane or behind hedges" who received that particular blessing, which was originally meant for me. I missed out.

I don't feel condemned over it, because I've asked forgiveness and His mercy is very great, but I sure learned from it and the other mistakes I've made. I never want to miss any surprise He has for me by hanging on to kryptonite.

When these unexpected invitations to receive His Word or wisdom come, and we drop all excuses to opt out, we will be strengthened. Remember, kryptonite only weakens us.

Sadly, some will continue to make excuses, time and time again. They will never make Him a priority and may miss out on the big banquet. I hope not since there is room in His house, and we are all invited.

Please pray this simple request I made so many years ago: *"Father, I ask in the name of Jesus Christ my Lord, that You would purify my heart. I want to be holy, set apart for You, so if there's anything in my life not pleasing to You or is a priority over You, expose it and help me remove it. I don't want to miss any of Your banquets!"*

TAKE ACTION

Hopefully, you already prayed the prayer at the end of this chapter. If you did, God will begin working in your life over the next few days, weeks, and months to draw you nearer to Him and, in the process, expose those things that keep you distant from Him. Engage this proactively right now by asking God to speak to you about anything in your life that has become an excuse to keep you from responding to His words. Write down what He reveals to you and take a few minutes to pray about them. Ask God for His perspective on those things and write what He tells you.

If you did not pray the prayer at the end of the chapter, take time right now to pray a different kind of prayer. Ask God to give you a willing and courageous heart so that you are able to pray that prayer. Write down anything God puts on your heart as you are praying.

27

THE BANQUET DOOR

Jesus makes the most remarkable statement to another church in the book of Revelation. His words closely resemble what we just discussed in the previous chapter:

> "Look! I stand at the door and knock. *If you hear* My voice and open the door, I will come in, and we will share a meal together as friends." (Revelation 3:20)

A banquet with Jesus! It's a fellowship feast—companionship with the Master. There we receive of His Word, wisdom, counsel, power, or any other wonderful blessings from His presence. Hopefully, such a meal creates hunger, anticipation, and excitement to receive from Him. This is what will strengthen us—a meal provided by Jesus is the very antithesis of kryptonite. It can be compared to Superman receiving renewed strength from the sun. Jesus is the living Word, the true Bread from heaven, and His presence gives us the strength to resist any form of kryptonite.

The question is, "What door is He knocking at?" Many ministers have used this Scripture to call people to salvation, and that's great. But we must remember He is addressing the church, His followers, not those who've never known Him. However, the crucial aspect of Jesus's statement doesn't center on the door. Rather, it's His words, "If you hear."

If I'm in my house with music blasting through my surround sound and an important visitor knocks at my door and calls out my name, I'm not going to hear. My guest will eventually leave.

So the more important question becomes, "What is keeping us from hearing?" If we don't hear, we miss out on the banquet, so let's look into and answer this vital question.

Holiness

If you mention the word "holiness" in the modern church, people often recoil and quickly change the topic. It's not cool for those who are "progressive" and supposedly puts a damper on life. All too often, holiness is viewed as synonymous to earning salvation through works or perceived as legalism.

However, it's the only description of the church Jesus is coming back for found in the New Testament. We are not told He's coming back for a "leadership-driven" church, a "relevant" church, a "connected" church, or one with a strong "community." All of these traits are extremely important to the growth and success of a church, but none of these is the defining characteristic of the bride of Christ.

Unfortunately, due to past legalistic preaching, many draw back from addressing holiness. To grow a large church today, it seems this topic needs to be avoided altogether. At the same time, observant leaders know that holiness is discussed throughout the New Testament, so the topic has to be addressed. Therefore, these communicators have made holiness more palatable with a doctrine stated something like this: "When it comes to holiness, we don't need to be concerned about personal responsibility, because Jesus is our holiness—it is secured in Christ." This doctrine is correct, but not completely so, because the New Testament speaks of two different aspects of holiness. Too much contemporary teaching and preaching lumps both into one bucket.

Regarding the first aspect of holiness, we are told:

God loved us and chose us in Christ *to be holy* and *without fault* in His eyes. (Ephesians 1:4)

Before we ever did anything worthy of eternal value, God made a decision. He chose us, and in doing so, He declared us holy. We are without fault in His eyes. This is "positional holiness." On the day we received Jesus, we became holy in God's sight, and we will never be more holy. Twenty-five million years from now, you'll be as holy then as the day you received Jesus.

To illustrate, I met Lisa Toscano in June of 1981. I fell in love with her shortly afterward and made a decision to marry her. On October 2, 1982, she became my wife. She is not more my wife today, thirty-five years later, than the day I married her. Nor will she be more my wife on our seventieth anniversary. She holds that *position* of being John Bevere's wife. She didn't have to earn it, work for it, or buy it. She is my wife because I chose her.

This is the holiness some leaders teach and it's true, but there's more. Let me use my marriage scenario again to illustrate the other aspect of holiness.

Before Lisa met me, she flirted with, gave her phone number to, and dated guys who she found interesting. After we got married, she stopped flirting with and pursuing other men. She now exudes a *behavior* that corresponds with the *position* she holds as my wife.

Look at the apostle Peter's words:

So you *must* live as God's obedient children. Don't slip back into your old ways of living to satisfy your own desires. You didn't know any better then. But now you *must* be holy in everything *you do*, just as God who chose you is holy. (1 Peter 1:14–15)

I've emphasized some words. First, notice the word *must*. What Peter is stipulating about behavior is not optional. Second, Peter is not talking about our *position* in Christ, but rather what *we do*. The *Amplified* version brings this out nicely: "You yourselves also be holy in all your *conduct* and *manner of living.*" This is *behavioral* holiness, not *positional.* It's similar to Lisa's change of behavior after we were married. Our behavior must reflect our position.

This is where the conflict begins. Earlier in my Christian life, I repeatedly tried to live holy and repeatedly failed. I was frustrated, to say the least. Then I discovered the grace of God. I found out grace is God's unmerited empowerment that gives us the ability to do what we couldn't do in our own ability. I couldn't get free from pornography and other sinful habits, but when I discovered grace, I was able to walk in freedom by believing and cooperating with it.

Here is a sad fact. Our ministry did a survey a few years back. We went to a variety of churches representing an array of doctrinal streams and denominations. We polled over five thousand born-again Christians across our nation. We asked participants to give three or more definitions of the grace of God. The survey results showed nearly everyone associated God's grace with salvation, forgiveness of sins, a free unmerited gift, and the love of God. This was the good news. The tragic result was less than two percent of those believers knew that grace is God's *empowerment.* Yet God Himself states, "'My *grace* is enough for you, *for My power* is made perfect in weakness'" (2 Corinthians 12:9 NET). He refers to His grace as His empowerment.

Peter writes, "May God give you more and more grace. . . . By His divine power, God has given us everything we need for living a godly life"

(2 Peter 1:2–3). Peter refers to God's grace as His divine power that gives us the ability to live godly—holy.

Reality is that we can't receive anything from God unless we believe. And we cannot believe what we do not know. If approximately two percent of American Christians know that grace empowers us, then roughly ninety-eight percent of American Christians are trying to live holy in their own ability, which is impossible. Frustration, defeat, depression, condemnation, and guilt are sure to follow this scenario.

Hence, the reason becomes clear why Christian communicators would lump all aspects of holiness into the *positional* category of holiness. Too many Christians have suffered discouragement from the lack of ability to live godly in their unaided strength. Grace is not only God's answer to salvation and forgiveness, but His powerful provision to live a holy life! The writer of Hebrews states:

> Pursue . . . holiness, without which no one will see the Lord: looking carefully lest anyone fall short of the grace of God. (Hebrews 12:14–15 NKJV)

There is so much in these two verses. First, the word "pursue" is the Greek word *dioko*. It is defined as "to follow or press hard after, to pursue with earnestness and diligence in order to obtain" (WSNTDICT). Another dictionary states: "To do something with intense effort and with definite purpose or goal" (LOUW-NIDA).

After reading these two definitions we should first ask, is this *positional* holiness or *behavioral* holiness? The answer is simple: It has to be *behavioral*. Look at it like this: Can you imagine saying to my wife, "Lisa Bevere, you need to apply intense effort to obtain the position of being John Bevere's wife."

She would laugh and say, "I'm already his wife."

In regard to *position*, we are already holy—we don't have to apply intense effort to chase after it. So the writer of Hebrews must be addressing *behavior*.

We are to pursue with diligence *behavioral* holiness. If we don't we will "fall short of the grace of God." How can we fall short of the cover-up grace that has been preached in our time? It would be impossible. Yet, when we understand grace is God's divine empowerment to chase after behavioral holiness, we can comprehend how we can fall short of this.

The writer of Hebrews ends this chapter with, "Let us have grace, by which we may serve God acceptably" (Hebrews 12:28 NKJV). Grace empowers us to serve God in an acceptable way and live a holy life.

Now comes the important part. We read, "Pursue . . . holiness, without which no one will *see the Lord*" (Hebrews 12:14 NKJV). What is this writer talking about? Isn't everyone going to see Jesus? We are clearly told, "Behold, He is coming with clouds, and *every eye will see Him*, even they who pierced Him" (Revelation 1:7 NKJV). So how can this Scripture communicate "without holiness we won't see the Lord"? What does this mean?

Seeing Jesus

Allow me to illustrate what "seeing the Lord" means, as promised in the pursuit of holiness. In my fifty-eight years of being an American citizen, there have been twelve presidents of the United States. I've been under the jurisdiction and leadership of all of them, and their decisions have affected my life. I've often referred to each of them as "our president." However, I've never *seen* one in person. There are other U.S. citizens who *see* the president on an ongoing basis since they are friends or work with him. These privileged ones *see* him regularly and are frequently in his *presence*.

Along these same lines, I've known a lot of facts down through the years about our U.S. presidents—what they stand for, the decisions they make, their personal history, and other information made known to the public. But what I have not been privy to is experiencing personal interaction with these leaders. Therefore, I'm unfamiliar with the intimate areas of their life—the things that aren't made known to the general public. And I've certainly never come close to having the pleasure of being a personal friend to one of them.

Similarly, there are Christians who are under the jurisdiction of Jesus. Because He is their Leader, His decisions affect their lives and they call Him "Lord," but they don't see Him and are not in His presence. You may question this, but allow me to have Jesus settle this truth:

> The person who has My commands and keeps them is the one
> who [really] loves Me; and whoever [really] loves Me will be loved
> by My Father, and I [too] will love him and will show (reveal,
> manifest) Myself to him. [I will let Myself *be clearly seen* by him
> and make Myself real to him.] (John 14:21 AMPC)

Look at His words, "let Myself be clearly *seen*.'" To have and keep Jesus's *commands* is to chase after behavioral holiness. These who do this *see the Lord*; He reveals Himself to them. He grants them access into His manifest *presence*. The relationship transcends from being merely under His rulership to the level of friendship with our King. He again says:

> You are My friends *if* you keep on doing the things which I command you to do. (John 15:14 AMPC)

Please notice the word "if" in His statement. We sing songs, write books, and teach messages about Jesus being our Friend. But the word "if" means His friendship is *conditional*. Friendship with Jesus is based on our genuine holiness, and those who make it a priority transcend from *servant* to *friend* status. Jesus says to the men who remained loyal to Him, "'No longer do I call you *servants*" (John 15:15 NKJV). The fact that He says "no longer" means at one time they were regarded as servants, not friends.

In fact, a servant of God isn't a bad position, and it's certainly much better than having no relationship with Him. However, a servant doesn't know the "why" behind the "what," but the friend often does.

You may counter, "But we are all sons and daughters of God." Yes, but we must remember the truth Paul shares that "the heir, as long as he is a child, does not differ at all from a *slave*" (Galatians 4:1 NKJV). The Greek word for "slave" is the exact same Greek word Jesus uses for the word "servant" in the above verse. As long as the son or daughter is a child, he or she normally is not privy to the why, just the *what* of God's doings.

It's a wonderful occurrence for both parent and child when a son or daughter graduates to becoming a friend. The same is true for the family of God. A change occurs in the relationship dynamic, as our Father lets us in on more secrets. But there's a change for us as well. We now live more passionately to not disappoint Him, much beyond just not disobeying Him. We still, and always will, seek to obey, but it's no longer our heart's driving force. Not disappointing Him is.

The Door

Holiness therefore is not an end in itself, as legalists portray it. It's the entranceway to true intimacy with Jesus. Now we discover the importance of the "door" that Jesus refers to: it's the heart of a believer. Our neglect to pursue holiness removes our ability to hear and respond. We subsequently lose the privilege of a feast with Him. It could be compared to a house so noisy that we can't hear when someone of great importance is knocking on the front door. After repeated knocks and even calling out our name, the desired guest eventually leaves.

In avoiding teaching on holiness, what we have done is block the pathway that leads to intimacy with our King, which is what every true believer desires more than anything else! Our strategy of teaching a *covering grace* that omits *empowering grace* has, in essence, shut the door and turned the deadbolt. We've undersold grace, for it both *covers* as well as *empowers*! However, the empowerment aspect is vital in positioning us to enjoy fellowship with the Master.

Lisa and I have a marriage certificate from the state of Indiana, so we are legally married. Can you imagine this scenario: I hold my marriage certificate up in her face and declare, "Hey, Honey, we are married, we are legally bound to each other, but I'm having affairs with other women." I may technically be married to Lisa, but it's certain she will no longer share her innermost desires and secrets with me. In fact, intimacy will cease. We will no longer be friends, because I will have lost that privilege. Is that a great life together? Is that what we got married for? If I persist on this course, I will eventually lose my marriage permanently.

Have we encouraged a similar behavior in what we've taught in the church? Do we hold up a few Scriptures that, if isolated from other sections of the New Testament, seem to show all is well no matter how we behave? Can we now jump in bed with the world while still declaring to Jesus, "We have *recited the sinner's prayer*, are *saved by grace*, and *belong to You*"? Can we possibly believe He will let us into the intimate parts of His heart?

The motivation for me to not commit adultery against Lisa is that I don't ever want to lose the wonder of those special, intimate times when our heads are on our pillow facing each other, and she whispers something to me that she would never tell anyone else. I don't want to lose the pleasure of these interactions with this remarkable woman who's my wife.

It's no different with Jesus. The reason I don't commit adultery against Him is that I don't want to lose our closeness and throw away our friendship. There is nothing greater, no status, no riches, no pleasure, no activity, no popularity, no position, no sin—nothing that's better than intimacy with Jesus.

I can't imagine life without His promise, "'I will tell you remarkable secrets you do not know'" (Jeremiah 33:3). Or the awesome reality that He "'reveals deep and secret things'" (Daniel 2:22 NKJV). Or I can't imagine living without Jesus's offer to, "'No longer speak . . . in figurative language, but I will tell you plainly'" (John 16:25 NKJV). And, of course, the promise of His Spirit showing us things to come (see John 16:13).

Holiness is not a negative; on the contrary, it's one of the most positive truths in the New Testament. When we really understand its potential, we shout it from the rooftops!

TAKE ACTION

Holiness isn't a bad word; it's a password. It is the way that enables you to open the door of your heart to God's voice. Without holiness, you won't even hear when He is speaking to you. This holiness is not just something God gives you because of Jesus's sacrifice; it is something you must—*must*—live out in thought, word, and action.

But it is not something God leaves you to struggle with alone. This is why God gives us grace! His grace does far more than just save us, though that much is amazing. God's grace empowers us to live holy lives from the inside out, fully pleasing to God!

Seek God right now. Don't wait any longer, but take this moment to cry out to God for His grace. Name the area of your life where you need His grace the most and pray that God would fill you with grace to overcome everything that hinders you from hearing His voice.

28

┌ ARISE ┘

Why are the superhero movies the most popular of all time? Think of it: These Hollywood productions attract more moviegoers than war movies, Westerns, espionage thrillers, and even love stories. And it's not just a guy thing, because I constantly meet women who profess their love for these blockbuster hits. Why is this? We know we were created for more, and our superheroes model our unspoken internal longings.

Think of Superman. When the impossible looms, overwhelming adversity arises, and all seems hopeless, immediately Clark Kent slips out of the *Daily Planet,* enters a phone booth and moments later, charges to the rescue. We love feeling the exhilarating sensation of him conquering enemies that seemed unstoppable. We're ecstatic when injustice is brought to a halt, victims are liberated, and society is put back into its right order.

It all comes down to this: We revel in our superheroes prevailing over evil, because it satisfies our innermost longing. We know that from the beginning God created human beings "godlike, reflecting God's nature" (Genesis 1:27 MSG). We also are told, "'The LORD is a warrior'" (Exodus 15:3). Have you thought much about this? It's the side of His nature that's rarely mentioned. It's almost as though we don't know what to do with this truth. Yet again, Isaiah declares:

The LORD will march forth like a mighty hero; He will come out
like a warrior, full of fury. He will shout His battle cry and crush
all His enemies. (Isaiah 42:13)

Warriors who fight injustice are heroes. In Jesus's case, He's the *true*
Superhero. He is the Conqueror and the Overcomer.

Long before Isaiah penned these words, Joshua saw Him. Our King
wasn't carrying a lamb, but instead a sword and identified Himself as "'the
Commander of the Lord's army'" (Joshua 5:14).

Long after Isaiah penned these words, the apostle John also saw the
Lord and described Him in an even more awesome way: "His eyes were
like flames of fire" and "from His mouth came a sharp sword" (Revelation
19:12–15).

He is a warrior! Most of us know a warrior isn't mild-mannered, sub-
dued, or melancholy by nature. No, a warrior in the midst of action is
focused, determined, and fierce.

Now let's turn our focus to us. Have you ever considered the fact that
Jesus says to all seven churches in the book of Revelation, something to
this effect: "To everyone who overcomes (or is victorious) . . . " How can
we be overcomers if there is nothing to overcome? How can we be victorious if there is no battle?

There are many today who downplay this calling. They say our identity in Christ makes us overcomers. In other words, because He is *the
Overcomer*, we are automatically overcomers in Christ. That's true in regard to our position in Him, but that's not the complete truth. Why would
Jesus say to the people in all seven churches "to the one who overcomes"
if it's automatic to our salvation?

There is a Lex Luthor in the universe and his name is Satan. He has a
host of cohorts who are not stupid, and their number one goal is to stop,
capture, and control you. To this end, Satan works 24/7. But he has been

"'As the Father has sent Me, so I am sending you'" (John 20:21). If that's not startling enough, He plainly says, "'I tell you the truth, anyone who believes in Me will do the same works I have done, and even greater works'" (John 14:12). The same works, and even greater! Is this possible? If He said it, absolutely yes! The early church experienced a good measure of this reality. They walked in such an authority, power, and boldness that entire towns and cities came to Jesus in just days. The same is also true of present-day occurrences I've witnessed or heard of.

In regard to the early church, if we consider just Jerusalem, no one in the city was unaffected. In just days, one of these three things transpired: Citizens were either stunned by the powerful events, angered by Jesus being proclaimed, or drawn into the kingdom. The church grew exponentially, operated in great power, and experienced several notable miracles. In one incident, a man lame from birth, who was carried to the meeting place daily, was healed. He instantly started jumping and shouting, and a good part of the city gathered and was amazed!

The authorities arrested Peter and John in attempts to thwart the building of the movement's momentum. They were brought before members of the council who concluded:

> Now when they saw the *boldness* of Peter and John, and perceived
> that they were uneducated and untrained men, they marveled. And
> they realized that *they had been with Jesus*. (Acts 4:13 NKJV)

Boldness is what caught the attention of the council. It would have been much easier for Peter and John to cower and pull a political maneuver of peacekeeping before the most influential men of the city. They could have refrained from the confrontation. However, they stayed true in the face of great danger.

What boldness and what strength—where did it come from? It's found in the words, "they had been with Jesus." These men had walked and were still walking in the presence of the Master. They did the same works He had done, which resulted in changed cities. They were men of holiness. The early church steered clear of kryptonite and chose to stay close to the Son—drawing their strength from Him. Therefore, they walked in great boldness, authority, and power.

Unfortunately, history also shows that the church in Corinth didn't impact their city, as the disciples did in Jerusalem and later in the cities of Samaria, Joppa, Lydda, Sharon, Antioch, and elsewhere throughout the regions of Judea and Asia. The Corinthian church was the antithesis. They were weak and void of the strength to impact their city. The amazing fact is the Corinthian church believed in and operated in the gifts of the Holy Spirit. Although a small measure of the miraculous occurred among these believers, they lacked what it took to impact their city.

What do we want for our generation? Is it possible to once again see cities impacted and changed? I'm invited to speak in many cities and celebrate the large attendance at many churches, but at the same time I grieve for the majority, sometimes millions of other people who are not being influenced for the kingdom. Why aren't we affecting towns, cities, and regions? Could it be that kryptonite has gained the upper hand?

God has revealed our destiny through the life of a judge in the Old Testament. His name is Samson. He flirted with disobedience until it became a pattern in his life. Eventually, Samson paid the awful price as kryptonite stole his strength. He could no longer operate with supernatural powers as he once had. However, after much suffering, he repented and his strength returned. In the end, he did greater feats than during all the years before he lost his strength.

The prophet Daniel foretells a generation who will not back down to any adversity in the final days. He prophesies:

> The people who *know their God* shall prove themselves strong and shall stand firm and do exploits [for God]. (Daniel 11:32 AMPC)

The key to this army's strength and power is they intimately "know their God." The key to this closeness is their pursuit of genuine holiness.

Final Words

So there it is. You are called by God to be a hero, a champion, one who wins in life and makes a difference in your world of influence. Be strong, be courageous, draw close to the King, because He desires you. He longs to be close to and empower you. He is for you. He believes in you and, most importantly, He loves you with an eternal love.

You are one of the true superheroes of this earth. Greater is our Champion who is within you than the Lex Luthor of this world. Draw strength from Him and change many lives. Your impact will not be fully known until you stand before the King's throne. You will be so glad both now and in that day that you didn't succumb to kryptonite.

So, kill kryptonite, destroy it, annihilate it, and don't give it any place—not even a slight opening—in your life. You were made for great glory and strength. Mighty one, you have a destiny, and this world needs you to fulfill it.

TAKE ACTION

God is a warrior, and we were made to be like Him. This is the reason superhero movies appeal so deeply to something inside of us. We know innately that we were born for greatness!

This is what God created you for, and we see testimonies throughout history of people who did marvelous acts for God when they left no room for the kryptonite of known sin in their lives. Cities have been transformed in a matter of days by the power of God and the boldness of His people. God is calling you to step up and be part of doing it again.

Ask God what battle He is calling you to fight. What city, region, territory, or nation is He calling you to reach? Write what you hear Him tell you and pray for God to pour His grace on you to accomplish His purpose there. Then fix your eyes on your eternal reward—the promise of all you will gain through your faithful, overcoming service in this life—and get going. God has called you to be a hero!

DISCUSSION
QUESTIONS

If you're reading this book as part of the *Killing Kryptonite* study or course (which is a really great idea!), I recommend that you watch each week's video lesson and unpack the corresponding discussion questions as a group. The video lessons will parallel and amplify major themes from this book, so it's ideal for all participants to both watch the lessons and read the book.

Enjoy!

Lesson 1: Our Potential

Highlights themes from chapters 1–3

1. You won't be motivated to tap into any potential you are unaware of. How have you seen this principle to be true in your life? What new products, technologies, or beliefs have you embraced after you found out what they could do for you? How is this similar to what you learned in this lesson?

2. Our potential in God includes nearly unimaginable possibilities. How did this lesson inspire you to explore the potential of your

identity in Christ? What are some areas where you've been thinking too small?

3.   Why do you think our potential in Christ is not commonly taught in churches today? How do you think the church would change if we were taught to believe all this was possible? As you meditate on these possibilities, how are they beginning to change you?

4.   When we fall so far short of what we as Christians could be, it affects how the world views both Christianity and God. How would the world look at Christians differently if we did fulfill our potential? How would they look at God differently if we fulfilled our potential?

Lesson 2: The Power of One

Highlights themes from chapters 4–7

1.   Paul writes that because the Corinthians didn't honor the body of Christ, many among them were weak, sick, and even dying prematurely. This still applies to us today, and it says it affected *many*. How is this different from what you have been taught about the church— the body of Christ? Why is this important for all believers to understand today?

2.   Many in the body of Christ fail to reach their potential because of known sin in the church, but this is not the only reason Christians get sick, die prematurely, or are weak. Why is it so important to make this distinction? What are some of the other reasons for afflictions within the church?

3.   In the West we have very individualistic mindsets, yet we see that when Achan sinned against God, all of Israel was affected because they were one body. How does this truth affect the way you view your role within the body of Christ?

4. Spiritual kryptonite is known sin. Achan knew it was wrong to take spoils for himself, and the Corinthians knew their drunkenness, gluttony, and selfishness during communion were also sin. Both instances caused weakness and death among those who did nothing wrong. Why do you think God takes sin in His body so seriously? Why do you think He wants us to place such a high value, not just on the individual believer, but on the body as a whole?

Lesson 3: Kryptonite

Highlights themes from chapters 8–10

1. Can you imagine a situation like Justin and Angela's actually happening? Of course you can't. But what similarities do you see to how some Christians treat their relationships with God? How would you respond to someone treating their spouse that way? How would you respond to someone treating God that way?
2. Known sin is spiritual kryptonite, and spiritual kryptonite is idolatry. What does it mean that so many churchgoers are actually worshiping idols? What does idolatry look like in a nation that doesn't bow down to statues and idols?
3. Idolatry is not something that's commonly taught in most churches. What stood out to you the most from what you learned in this lesson about idolatry? Why do you think that stood out to you the most?
4. Consistently throughout Scripture, God equates idolatry with adultery. In your own words, why do you think God does this? What does it say about the relationship He offers us?
5. Idolatry begins by worshiping creation rather than its Creator. What is God's response to this behavior? Why would God distance Himself from those who don't choose Him? Why do you think an affinity

toward homosexuality is a telltale sign that a society has embraced idolatry?

6. If we're going to recognize idolatry, we have to understand true worship. True worship is obedience to God's commands, not singing a slow song. How does this understanding of worship change the way you think about Christian living? Who have you seen in your life who has given you the best example of a lifestyle of worshiping God?

Lesson 4: Modern Idolatry

Highlights themes from chapters 11–14

1. The story of Saul's disobedience when saving some of the Amalekites shows us the root of idolatry in the church. How is Saul's covetousness equal to idolatry?
2. Samuel told Saul that stubbornness is the same as idolatry. This is when we cling to what we want over what God has declared to be His will. And, as we see in Saul's life, it opened the door to much greater sin in his life. How is this idolatry? Why does it lead to greater sins?
3. Covetousness is what leads us into idolatry and, in fact, is idolatry in itself. But contentment is what leads to godliness. When you look at your own goals, priorities, and habits, which would you say is stronger in your life—covetousness or contentment? How can you pursue a life of greater contentment?
4. While contentment is necessary in every Christian's life, we cannot confuse it with complacency. In your own words, how are these two different? How would you know if someone was content, but not complacent?

5. Another important clarification to remember is that idolatry is never when a believer falls into sin, but only when they are given over to sin. According to all you've learned so far in these lessons, how can you tell the difference between these two?

6. If we're going to understand that willful sin is spiritual kryptonite, we have to also understand that God offers us a completely new life with a new nature—His nature. Have you realized that it's possible to not be prone to sin, but to instead be prone to righteousness? How does it make you feel to know this transformation is possible—and even expected of your life?

Lesson 5: A Knockoff Jesus

Highlights themes from chapters 15–18

1. God's purpose in saving you was to bring you to Himself. He wants to be in intimate relationship with you. This requires you to wash yourself of the things of the world, because He wants an authentic relationship with you. What does this mean? How can you know that you have done this?

2. Imagine God's disappointment when people He longs to bring to Himself refuse to come to Him, even after they claim to be saved by Him. How would you feel if you married someone, but they refused to be in the same room as you? What if they wouldn't even talk on the phone with you? What if they would only relate to you through another person? What sort of relationship would you have with them after all that?

3. Aaron remained in the camp, so we might say he was more comfortable in the camp with the people than in the presence of God on the mountain. Some people are this way—more comfortable in church

than in God's presence. How do you respond when you sense God's presence?

4. Israel had a high priest, declared *Yahweh* had delivered them from Egypt, and worshipped *Yahweh* with burnt offerings and sacrifices, all the while focusing this attention toward a golden calf—all for the sake of pursuing their own desires. If Israel could declare all these things with the right name, yet still have false, abominable worship, can today's church do the same? What would that look like?

5. Israel obeyed some of God's commandments, but neglected others. Churches all over the world do this same thing, choosing passages they like while ignoring the ones that challenge us to live holy lives, fully devoted to God. How can we know we are worshiping the true Jesus, not a knockoff Jesus?

Lesson 6: The Starting Place

Highlights themes from chapters 19–21

How did a knockoff *Yahweh* evolve in Israel, and how does a knockoff Jesus evolve in the church? Both are the result of a hardened heart from the absence of true repentance.

1. This lesson covers a lot about repentance—the necessity of it, its role in the gospel, and what it really means. How was this similar to or different from the way you've thought about repentance in the past? Does this change the way you think about the gospel? If so, how?

2. Every gospel begins with the story of John the Baptist, who preached repentance from sins. This means the gospel of Jesus always begins with repentance. How do you feel about this statement? Why is repentance so important to the gospel?

3. There is no true faith in Jesus Christ without repentance from known sin. If we cling to sin and claim to be Christians, then we are deceived. Why do you think God would care so much about how we live?

4. Remember the story of Justin and Angela, how Angela had no idea she was supposed to leave her boyfriends behind when she got married? How are all these people who don't know Jesus supposed to know they need to repent unless we tell them? What might happen to us if we tell people to stop sinning? Why is it important to count the cost of sharing the full gospel?

5. We are defined by our actions, not by our intentions. This shows the power of the gospel, that it can transform our entire person. How does this show that repentance is a positive and good thing? In your own words, explain how God's requirement for repentance is actually His mercy to us.

Lesson 7: Truth, Tolerance & Love

Highlights themes from chapters 22–24

1. Jude wanted to write about the wonder of our salvation—or the nice things—but had to warn his audience about people who were turning God's grace into a license for sin. In your own life, have you allowed yourself to neglect God's warnings, only saying the nice things? Why is it important for you to keep the warnings a part of your life and speech?

2. The reason the church has become tolerant toward sin is that we have a misguided understanding of what true love is. True love requires the truth, and the truth is always an eternal perspective. How does keeping an eternal perspective change what is important in your life?

3. The love of God means obeying God's commands. This is what distinguishes Christian love from worldly love. Without God's commands, how would you describe any difference between God's love and the world's love?

4. Love without the truth of God attached to it is not true love—it's a counterfeit. Our culture is walking away from this love, and that is why the church is motivated toward a knockoff Jesus. How do you feel about speaking the truth in love? Why do you think so many people are uncomfortable with the truth?

Lesson 8: Killing Kryptonite

Highlights themes from chapters 25–28

1. Some believers overlook sin because they are unaware of the reality that their sin hurts God's heart. Other Christians believe the lie that we are just sinners by nature and the blood of Jesus is powerful enough to set us free from the penalty of sin, but cannot free us from the bondage of sin. These are the believers with kryptonite—known, practiced sin. How has either of these beliefs influenced your life? How have you seen them influence other professing believers?

2. A third group of believers are genuine Christians who knowingly sin, but for them it is a constant struggle. They want to get out, but have not yet discovered from God's Word how to live free from sin. The shame of their sin holds them in their sin. What truths from this lesson would you share with a believer in this condition?

3. In this lesson, I share from my testimony of how God set me free from lust and pornography. What inspired you the most from this testimony? Why? What challenged you the most? Why?

4. Freedom from sin comes from godly sorrow, not from worldly sorrow. Godly sorrow recognizes the pain our sin causes God, but

worldly sorrow is only worried about how our sin affects us and our future. Why do you think God would only release grace to set us free with one kind of sorrow, but not the other? How would you tell the difference between these two sorrows in your own life?

5. So many superhero stories capture our imaginations because they connect with a longing in every human heart. The early believers were the superhumans of their day. How can we become the superhumans of our day? How would this change the way the world thinks about God?

6. God is a warrior, and we were created to be like Him. Jesus called all seven churches in Revelation to overcome, which means we are called to victory and we have an enemy to overcome. As you reflect on this entire message, how has it changed the way you think about what God calls you to overcome in this life? How has it changed the way you view yourself, other believers, and the church as a whole?

SALVATION, AVAILABLE TO ALL

If you openly declare that Jesus is Lord and believe
in your heart that God raised Him from the dead,
you will be saved. For it is by believing in your heart
that you are made right with God, and it is by openly
declaring your faith that you are saved.

ROMANS 10:9–10

God wants you to experience life in its fullness. He's passionate about you and the plan He has for your life. But there's only one way to start the journey to your destiny: by receiving salvation through God's Son, Jesus Christ.

Through the death and resurrection of Jesus, God made a way for you to enter His kingdom as a beloved son or daughter. The sacrifice of Jesus on the cross made eternal and abundant life freely available to you. Salvation is God's gift to you; you cannot do anything to earn or deserve it.

To receive this precious gift, first acknowledge your sin of living independently of your Creator, for this is the root of all the sins you have committed. This repentance is a vital part of receiving salvation. Peter made this clear on the day that five thousand were saved in the book of Acts: "Repent therefore and be converted, that your sins may be blotted out" (Acts 3:19 NKJV). Scripture declares that each of us is born a slave to sin. This slavery is rooted in the sin of Adam, who began the pattern of willful disobedience. Repentance is a choice to walk away from obedience to yourself and Satan, the father of lies, and to turn in obedience to your new Master, Jesus Christ—the One who gave His life for you.

You must give Jesus the lordship of your life. To make Jesus "Lord" means you give Him ownership of your life (spirit, soul, and body)—everything you are and have. His authority over your life becomes absolute. The moment you do this, God delivers you from darkness and transfers you to the light and glory of His kingdom. You simply go from death to life—you become His child!

If you want to receive salvation through Jesus, pray these words:

God in Heaven, I acknowledge that I am a sinner and have fallen short of Your righteous standard. I deserve to be judged for eternity for my sin. Thank You for not leaving me in this state, for I believe You sent Jesus Christ, Your only begotten Son, who was born of the virgin Mary, to die for me and carry my judgment to the Cross. I believe He was raised again on the third day and is now seated at Your right hand as my Lord and Savior. So on this day, I repent of my independence from You and give my life entirely to the Lordship of Jesus.

Jesus, I confess you as my Lord and Savior. Come into my life through Your Spirit and change me into a child of God. I renounce the things of darkness which I once held on to, and from this day forward I will no longer live for myself. By Your grace, I will live for You who gave Yourself for me that I may live forever.

Thank You, Lord; my life is now completely in Your hands and according to Your Word, I shall never be ashamed. In Jesus's name, Amen.

Welcome to the family of God! I encourage you to share your exciting news with another believer. It's also important that you join a Bible-believing local church and connect with others who can encourage you in your new faith. Feel free to contact our ministry (visit MessengerInternational.org) for help finding a church in your area.

You have just embarked on the most remarkable journey. May you grow in revelation, grace, and friendship with God every day!

KILLING KRYPTONITE

STAY ENGAGED WITH
KILLING KRYPTONITE
AND JOHN BEVERE

#KILLINGKRYPTONITE
JOHNBEVERE.COM

Connect with John on:

BOOKS BY JOHN

A Heart Ablaze
The Bait of Satan*
Breaking Intimidation*
Drawing Near
Driven by Eternity*
Enemy Access Denied
Extraordinary*
The Fear of the Lord*
Good or God?*
The Holy Spirit: An Introduction*

Honor's Reward*
How to Respond When You Feel Mistreated
Killing Kryptonite*
Relentless*
Rescued
The Story of Marriage*
Thus Saith the Lord?
Under Cover*
Victory in the Wilderness
The Voice of One Crying

Available in curriculum format

Messenger International exists to develop
uncompromising followers of Christ who
transform our world.

Call: 1-800-648-1477

Visit us online at: **MessengerInternational.org**

Connect with John Bevere:

JohnBevere.com